Clarifying McLuhan

CLARIFYING MCLUHAN

An Assessment of Process and Product

S. D. Neill

CONTRIBUTIONS TO THE STUDY OF MASS MEDIA
AND COMMUNICATIONS,
NUMBER 37

GREENWOOD PRESS

Westport, Connecticut • London

Library of Congress Cataloging-in-Publication Data

Neill, S. D. (Samuel D.), 1928–1992.
   Clarifying McLuhan : an assessment of process and product / S. D. Neill.
      p.   cm. — (Contributions to the study of mass media and communications, ISSN 0732–4456 ; no. 37)
   Includes bibliographical references and index.
   ISBN 0–313–28444–X (alk. paper)
      1. McLuhan, Marshall, 1911–1980. 2. Mass media.   I. Title.
   II. Series.
   P92.5.M3N4   1993
   302.23'092—dc20   92–36609

British Library Cataloguing in Publication Data is available.

Library of Congress Catalog Card Number: 92–36609
ISBN: 0–313–28444–X
ISSN: 0732–4456

First published in 1993

Greenwood Press, 88 Post Road West, Westport, CT 06881
An imprint of Greenwood Publishing Group, Inc.

Printed in the United States of America

The paper used in this book complies with the Permanent Paper Standard issued by the National Information Standards Organization (Z39.48–1984).

10 9 8 7 6 5 4 3 2 1

Acknowledgments

S. D. Neill, "McLuhan's media charts related to the process of communication," *AV Communication Review*, 21:3, Fall 1973, pp. 277–97, reproduced here as Appendix II, is reprinted by permission of the Association for Educational Communications and Technology, Washington, D.C. Copyright 1973.

Thanks to the anonymous reader for *Queen's Quarterly* who, several years ago now, made astute suggestions regarding parts of what is here Chapter 7, "The Artist as Antenna," thus enhancing the value of the peer review system of quality control in scholarly communication.

Thanks also to Barrington Nevitt for conversations about the ideas in this book.

To Herbert Marshall McLuhan who, other than Mary, had the sharpest intellect of anyone I have known, and who, as well, always warmly welcomed me—although Mary beat him there, too.

Contents

Contents   ix

Preface

Now, what I want is, Facts.

        (Thomas Gradgrind in Charles Dickens's *Hard Times*)

Since McLuhan's death there have been no major re-assessments, nor have his ideas found any serious expansion, deliberation or exegesis. To my knowledge no one has set to work finding experimental proof for any of his hypotheses.

        (William Kuhns, 1989)

Interestingly, his last book, the still unpublished *Laws of the Media*, is the most direct and logically organized of any of his published work. It is as though he wanted to make sure that he wouldn't be distracted by anything but the pure ideas. On the last occasion on which we met I read the book in manuscript form and told him that I thought it would stand with the *Gutenberg Galaxy* and *Understanding Media* as the best example of his work. Although he couldn't speak at the time, he nodded his head enthusiastically.

        (John Culkin, 1989)

I began this book as a critique of *Laws of Media: The New Science* (McLuhan and McLuhan, 1988). However, since *Laws* is a culmination of all of Marshall McLuhan's work, it was impossible to critique *Laws* without examining the basic tenets that were its foundation. This work is therefore a critical exegesis and assessment of the McLuhan message, concluding with an evaluation of McLuhan as the serious artist he claimed to be.

For anyone who has spent more than forty years in the company of McLuhan's writing and conversation, as I have (see Appendix I for a brief personal memoir), it was important to get away from the hypnotic rhythms and catchy phrases for a few years in order to bring a measure of objectivity to the task of analysis. Indeed, I began to realize some years ago that there was a real danger that I could begin to sound just like McLuhan, as his close collaborators often did. However, I had never been *completely* sure I knew what he was saying, and so "left his company" in the late 1970s, not to read his work again until the publication of *Laws of Media*.

When I came to the point of trying to clarify McLuhan, I realized early on that I would have to be selective. First of all, I avoided reading great stretches of his prose, for I knew how mesmerizing that could be. I had already read all of his books and many of his articles. I had published reviews of *Understanding Media* (McLuhan, 1946; see Neill, 1964b) and *Take Today* (McLuhan and Nevitt, 1972; see Neill, 1973b). Now I went step by step through *Laws* and referred back for confirmation and elaboration, mainly to *Understanding Media*.

The next decision was to choose examples from the numerous inaccurate statements, contradictions, and exaggerations; for it was clear it would be counterproductive to try for comprehensiveness. Indeed, as soon as McLuhan is seen as an artist rather than as a scientist or even a scholar (although he was a scholar in his own way), those irritating and confusing aspects become less important—important to recognize, but less important. They have to be *met* by anyone examining McLuhan's overall purpose before they can be moved aside.

Bibliographical Note

With the publication of *Understanding Media* in 1964 (McLuhan, 1964b), McLuhan's message was complete until *Laws of Media* came out eight years after his death in 1980 (see the last paragraph below). The books about McLuhan were clustered around the year 1970, with the exception of Philip Marchand's excellent (and fair) biography in 1989 and the commemorative (and friendly) collection by George Sanderson and Frank Macdonald, also in 1989.

Of the earliest works, three were collections of essays and reviews with the inclusion of a few pieces by McLuhan himself (Stearn, 1967; Crosby and Bond, 1968; and Rosenthal, 1968). Sidney Finkelstein (1968) wrote a short, popular, well-argued attack on McLuhan, whom Finkelstein labeled "spokesman for the Corporate Establishment." Dennis Duffy's (1969) little assault, about sixty pages in length, was part of a series on Canadian writers.

The two most scholarly works were Donald Theall's *The Medium Is the Rear View Mirror* (1971) and Toby Goldberg's unpublished dissertation "An Examination, Critique and Evaluation of the Mass Communications Theories of Marshall McLuhan" (1971). Theall's knowledge of the literary works McLuhan constantly cited gave him an avenue of criticism not available to others and his analysis of the individual works of McLuhan is still useful. Goldberg covered all the issues, including some touched on by Theall; but Goldberg's is an excellent compilation and source to the literature about McLuhan—both for and against—up to that point.

Marchand's biography and also the notes to *Letters of Marshall Mc-*

Luhan—published in 1987 by Matie Molinaro, McLuhan's agent, Corinne McLuhan, his wife, and William Toye, then the editorial director of Oxford Canada—are essential background for any study of McLuhan's work.

Laws of Media lists Eric McLuhan as coauthor—and rightly so, for Eric worked on the development of the material with his father for many years. He then completed the manuscript from Marshall McLuhan's notes and saw the book through the publication process. The ideas are, however, those of the elder McLuhan and it is with those ideas that I contend; so I will refer to them, and to *Laws of Media*, as "McLuhan's" rather than "McLuhan and McLuhan's," and will cite the book as *Laws of Media* or *Laws* for the sake of convenience.

1

Falsifying the Basic Theory

MCLUHAN ADOPTS POPPER

For some reason, Marshall McLuhan was anxious to be scientific—perhaps to overcome the guru image by proving there was more to his pronouncements than one individual's peculiar insights. Despite his flamboyant style, McLuhan was sincere and seriously concerned that he be understood.

He had confronted the need to create "testable hypotheses" (Neill, 1973a, p. 281; reprinted here as Appendix II) when he was contracted to study the media by the National Association of Educational Broadcasters in 1959. This contract resulted in the unpublished *Report on Project in Understanding New Media* (McLuhan, 1960a). The substance of that report was delivered at a conference in 1960 and published in the journal *AV Communication Review* (McLuhan, 1960b). After this presentation McLuhan dropped the "testable hypotheses" facet and reverted to his own literary, poetic and notably unscientific style.

Throughout the 1970s he and his son Eric, and others, worked on formulating the laws of the media, the earliest publication of this work being in German (McLuhan and McLuhan, 1974), followed by a brief presentation in the *Journal of Culture and Technology* (McLuhan, 1975). At the same time, McLuhan was looking for what it is that constitutes a scientific statement. He found what he wanted in Karl Popper's *Objective Knowledge* (1972)—that it is something stated in such a way that it can be "disproved" (*Laws*, p. viii; see the Bibliographical Note preceding this chapter).

Popper's approach was to lay stress on "negative arguments, such as negative instances or counter-examples" (1972, p. 20). A hypothesis claiming 'all swans are white' can be falsified by finding one (negative instance) black swan. With McLuhan's adoption of Popper's principle, I decided to apply it to the conjecture 'the medium is the message.' I have used two cases: T. S. Eliot's perception of simultaneity, and the effect of language script (the Chinese ideogram) on thought and culture.

THE CASE OF T. S. ELIOT'S PERCEPT OF SIMULTANEITY

When McLuhan said Eliot and Baudelaire and others were aware of and influenced by the "service environment of electric information" (*Laws*, p. 47), several examples were given to 'prove' the point. One was a few lines from "Burnt Norton" to show how Eliot articulated the "percept of simultaneity" (*Laws*, p. 47). Eliot speculated that the present and the past could be present in the future, and the future in the past. That is, all times are (eternally) present. Things that have been and things that might have been are all somehow connected to the present.

Here we have an opportunity to illustrate the Popperian criterion for what makes a scientific statement—falsifiability. The conjecture is that Eliot could not have written those lines about all times being present— that is, simultaneous—without electric sensibility. The conjecture can be falsified if even only one example can be found that shows a perception of all time being simultaneous that was written *before* the new electric sensibility.

McLuhan dated the electric information media from the development of the telegraph, patented 1837. Since much preliminary work preceded that event, we would be safer to begin our search from the seventeenth rather than the nineteenth century. The best example we find is Petrarch's sonnet "La vita fugge." I give the first four lines in translation.

> Life passes quick, nor will a moment stay,
> And death, with hasty journeys still draws near;
> And all the present joins my soul to tear,
> With every past and every future day:
>
> (Petrarca, 1879 [14th century])

The relevant lines are the third and fourth. Various other translations keep the same sense.

Petrarch was born in 1304 and died in 1374. I was not surprised to read Thomas Bergin's remarks about Petrarch, for they could apply equally as well to Eliot: "the melancholy observer of the contemporary, the not-quite-cloistered scholar" (Bergin, 1966, p. vii).

There is also an element of simultaneity in Lady Macbeth's speech (act 1, sc. 5, l. 58) addressing Macbeth after she has decided to kill Duncan.

> Great Glamis! worthy Cawdor!
> Greater than both, by the all-hail hereafter!
> Thy letters have transported me beyond
> This ignorant present, and I feel now
> The future in the instant.
>
>   (Shakespeare, 1904 [1606])

In these lines, the past is excluded, so *all* time is not "in the instant."

Abraham Cowley seems to be on the mark in the following lines from his poem "Davideis" (bk. 1, l. 360), first published in 1656 but written between 1636 and 1639 when he was a student at Cambridge.

> No circling *Motion* doth swift *Time* divide;
> Nothing there is *To Come*, and nothing Past,
> But an *Eternal Now* does always last.
>
>   (Cowley, 1707, p. 302)

However, it might be argued that the concept of all time being simultaneous is not present in these lines—that Cowley has not perceived simultaneity; that the concept here is that there is *no* time. It is, after all, a description of Heaven. On the other hand, Eliot's words *eternally present* are not far from the Eternal Now. Eliot chose to use "eternally" as a descriptor. He could have said "if all time is present," and not brought in the idea of eternity at all.

Staffan Bergsten, who discussed the time element more comprehensively than other readers of Eliot, commented:

Against this notion of temporality of things and events, implied in immediate experience as well as physics, Eliot sets the idea of co-existence of the past and future, of beginning and end. This idea is not original, however, not one invented by Eliot, as he was no doubt aware in using it. It goes back to Latin and Greek philosophy, and, emerging at intervals through the history of Western philosophy, it was subject to renewed discussion during the first decades of the present century. (Bergsten, 1960, p. 95)

Bergsten then referred to examples, particularly to Saint Augustine's *Confessions*. In Bergsten, the Eternal Now (*nunc stans*) is described as "a rigidly unredeemable simultaneity" (1960, p. 98).

Perhaps we can close this section with the words of Marcus Aurelius Antoninus, who died in A.D. 180, which offer another perception of simultaneity uninfluenced by electric information media.

Think what a multitude of events, corporeal and psychic alike, take place within each of us during the same infinitesimal portion of time; and it will seem to thee no marvel that far more things—nay, all that comes into being in that One and All which we call the Universe—should exist therein at once. (Antoninus, 1906, p. 72)

If I am right, then the basic theory of psychic transformation as a result of media impact does not hold and is invalidated. The entire McLuhan oeuvre is called into question if the criterion of falsifiability is used as the criterion of science.

If I am wrong, does McLuhan's conjecture hold? Since no empirical evidence has been presented to link with the electric media Eliot's conceptualization of his percept of simultaneous time, the conjecture would remain just that. It is also a weak conjecture since a more plausible explanation can be found in the circumstances surrounding the composition of the lines. Taking Popper as the arbiter, we know he thought that any "novel theory in physics is accepted only if it is thought to have empirical content in excess of that of prevailing theories" (Murdoch, 1987, p. 18). If one is going to be scientific by applying the criterion of falsifiability, then the criterion of empirical content can also be invoked.

Suffice it to say that Eliot had—long before the writing of "Burnt Norton," the quartet from which the lines are taken—discussed the effect of new poetry on old. In a segment from *Tradition and the Individual Talent*, which was published in 1917 and later included in Eliot's *Points of View* (1941), we read this: "What happens when a new work of art is created is something that happens simultaneously to all the works of art which preceded it" (1941, p. 25–26). He was aware that past literature was reordered by present literature and that future literature would do the same to present literature. Eliot had already thought about the interrelationship between past, present, and future from the standpoint of literature.

Just prior to the writing of "Burnt Norton," in the fall of 1935, Eliot had undergone a divorce and had also been to America to deliver the lectures that became *The Use of Poetry and the Use of Criticism* (1933). He was meditating on the problem of *Murder in the Cathedral*, which was produced in 1935 and from which the "simultaneity" lines had been rejected, later to reemerge in "Burnt Norton." Helen Gardner wrote, "It was a time of painful reflection on what had been and on what might have been" (1978, p. 31). For a philosophical person such as Eliot, the lines do not seem psychologically or intellectually discordant. Nor can we ignore Eliot's knowledge of the philosophical and religious literature, both contemporary and classical, that discussed the idea of time and of the Eternal Now (Bergsten, 1960). Further, Einstein's conception of time as a fourth dimension had caught the popular imagination early in the century, producing in the 1920s a large number of works on the notion of time (Bergsten, 1960). There is little doubt that Eliot's intellectual and psychological makeup are sufficient "reasons" for the content of his thought. Poets generally think in and look for universals; neither technology nor language can prevent that.

THE CASE OF THE CHINESE IDEOGRAM

McLuhan used various aspects of human culture to prove his point that the script of a language (alphabet, ideogram) causes radically different ways of viewing the world. The effects of the ideogram on the Chinese, he said, include: no individualism or point of view, a feeling of the oneness or unity and harmony of all things, the use of empty spaces in art as "resonant intervals" to get in touch with situations. The Chinese, as the "East," were unable to conceptualize the abstractions of space and time and so they "never had a Euclid" (*Laws*, p. 43).

No evidence is given for the statement. Indeed, A. C. Graham, in his careful and scholarly analysis of philosophical argument in ancient China, showed that, in the fifth century B.C., canons of the Mohists, space and time were in fact "fully abstracted" (1989, pp. 142, 427–28).

The existence of individual points of view is illustrated by the variety of schools of thought in ancient China, some of which, Graham notes, "are very much more rational than they used to look" (1989, p. 7). Indeed, the preaching of the Confucians was necessary because people were not doing what they ought to have been doing. During the third century B.C., Graham tells us, "as the intensifying struggle between the states approached its final crisis, rulers were hardly pretending any longer to listen to the moralising of the Confucians" (p. 267). Other works attesting to varieties of philosophical points of view are those of Herbert A. Giles (1915), Hu Shih (1963 [1922]), and Kam Louie (1980).

McLuhan used *The Book of Tea* by Okakura-Kakuzo (1912) as one of his sources for the view of the Oriental mind in harmony with the universe. Somehow, he missed the following sentence:

It should be remembered in the first place that Taoism, like its legitimate successor Zennism, represents the *individualistic* trend of the Southern Chinese mind in contra-distinction to the communism of Northern China which expressed itself in Confucianism. (Okakura-Kakuzo, 50–51, my emphasis)

Tea drinking as a cult spread early in Japan. Rand Castile (1971) described the life of the priest Eison who, from A.D. 1239 went about the country preaching Zen and "teaism."

One story of the time tells of Eison approaching a shepherd with an offering of tea. The shepherd inquired as to the nature of the beverage, and Eison assured him that it contained the very gift of enlightenment, for it prevented sleep and destroyed the passions. The shepherd gently refused the priest's tea, for, he said, "in my job I must work very hard—therefore I need my sleep and as I have nothing else for pleasure I cannot refuse my passions. If tea rids me of both, then I shall have none of it." (Castile, 1971, p. 40)

The point is that individualistic points of view existed in the East as well as in the West.

If language (whether oral or ideogramic) eliminates individualism from a particular culture, and if that culture also teaches communal and family reverence, *no one* would ever be individualistic. On the other hand, if these characteristics were merely historical and cultural (rather than "psychic"), then individual minds would be free to rebel or at least differ—which seems to be the case. Chinese communist morality, enforced on top of the proposed McLuhanist effect of language, has failed to squelch individual acts of rebellion as was seen in the phenomenon of Tiananmen Square. Richard Madsen's study (1984) of two Chinese village leaders, only one of whom was literate, provides a good example of the existence of individualism in spite of the weight of centuries of culture and of political overseers, or "work teams." On one occasion when, for his bad behavior, one of the leaders was locked in a cowshed, the work team announced that he would be released and not punished if he confessed his guilt. The following describes his confession.

He wept and cursed himself. He apologized with shame to Chairman Mao. He said that Liu Sheoqi had harmed him, that he had become gravely individualistic. He hadn't been able to get rid of his individualism. When he had fallen, he had been very discontented and had wanted to harm other people, so that he would have a chance to "ascend the stage again." (Madsen, 1984, p. 209)

The existence of the concept of individualism is telling enough in itself.

Saying that individualism was present in Chinese culture does not mean that it ever succeeded in dominating that culture. Clearly it did not. In classical Confucianism, the sort of individualism prized in the West—the individual as a separate entity from the political body—would be completely undesirable, even barbaric. David Hall and Roger Ames, in their controversial analysis of Confucius, warn that "the very notion of 'individual' in the strictest sense is suspect from the Confucian perspective. 'Sociality' is at the very root of existence" (1987, p. 153). It is necessary to remember, however, that Confucius was an *advocate* of a social and behavioral order. Many did not understand him; hence the dialogs (like those of Socrates) designed to get his teachings across. Hall and Ames remind us of his failure to convert everyone (in spite of the ideogram): "In an effort to bring harmony to a world writhing in internecine warfare, he embarked on a thirteen-year tour of the central states at the end of his life" (p. 308).

On the other hand, a version of Confucianism was so pervasive that Chinese culture was parochial and isolationist. For Hall and Ames, this was a failing in imagination (p. 311). The Confucian position

fairly understood requires that the prevailing norms remain ever open to ne-
gotiating novel circumstances. At least theoretically, the patternings of these
norms are in fact enhanced by an increasing degree of difference. This, then,
has been another failure of the Confucian tradition. Confucianism has historically
been prone to ossify and become an ideology. (Hall and Ames, 1987, p. 310)

What does this mean in the context of linguistic influence? If the
language has the causal effect on perception and thinking that McLuhan
said it has, every Chinese person would think the same—all like
Confucius.

Unity and Harmony

McLuhan's perception of the Eastern world view came in part from
Fritjof Capra's book *The Tao of Physics* (1975). The most important characteristic of this view is

the awareness of the unity and mutual interrelation of all things and events,
the experience of all phenomena in the world as manifestations of a basic oneness. All things are seen as interdependent and inseparable parts of this cosmic
whole; as different manifestations of the same ultimate reality. (Capra, 1975,
p. 133, quoted in *Laws*, p. 43)

Seeing all things as one and in harmony is not just an Eastern philosophy. Mystics and poets of all languages express that insight or desire.
Indeed, Capra himself says as much:

This view is not limited to the East, but can be found to some degree in all
mystically oriented philosophies. The argument of this book could therefore be
phrased more generally, by saying that modern physics leads us to a view of
the world which is very similar to the views held by mystics of all ages and
tradition. (Capra, 1975, p. 19)

The nineteenth-century transcendentalists were very good at it. Ralph
Waldo Emerson is a good example. Here are two quotations from his
essay "Nature":

Who looks upon a river in a meditative hour, and is not reminded of the flux
of all things? Throw a stone into a stream, and the circles that propagate themselves are the beautiful type of all influence. Man is conscious of a universal
soul within or behind his individual life, wherein, as in a firmament, the natures
of Justice, Truth, Love, Freedom, arise and shine. . . .
    Herein is especially apprehended the unity of Nature—the unity of variety—
which meets us everywhere. All the endless variety of things make an identical
impression. Xenophanes complained in his old age, that look where he would,
all things hastened back to unity. He was weary of seeing the same entity in

the tedious variety of forms. The fable of Proteus has a cordial truth. A leaf, a drop, a crystal, a moment of time is related to the whole, and partakes of the perfection of the whole. Each particle is a microcosm, and faithfully renders the likeness of the world. (Emerson, n.d., pp. 12, 21)

Emerson was thirty-four when the telegraph was invented in 1837, although his dominant medium of communication was—other than his voice—the printed (alphabetic) work. Nevertheless, it might be safer to present an instance of the perception of universal harmony from the eighteenth century. William Wordsworth's "Tintern Abbey," written in 1798, includes the following lines.

> For I have learned
> To look on nature, not as in the hour
> Of thoughtless youth; but hearing oftentimes
> The still, sad music of humanity,
> Nor harsh nor grating, though of ample power
> To chasten and subdue, And I have felt
> A presence that disturbs me with the joy
> Of elevated thoughts; a sense sublime
> Of something far more deeply interfused,
> Whose dwelling is the light of setting suns,
> And the round ocean, and the living air,
> And the blue sky, and in the mind of man,
> A motion and a spirit, that impels
> All thinking things, all objects of all thought,
> And rolls through all things.
>
> (Wordsworth, 1891 [1798], pp. 206–7)

At various times, even ordinary, everyday people feel this unity and the need of it, but do not (or cannot) express it. We can add to the evidence the previously quoted words of Marcus Aurelius Antoninus, which apply equally well to this context.

Think what a multitude of events, corporeal and psychic alike, take place within each of us during the same infinitesimal portion of time; and it will seem to thee no marvel that far more things—nay, all that comes into being in that One and All which we call the Universe—should exist therein at once. (Antoninus, 1906, p. 76)

Painting

Chiang Yee's book, *The Chinese Eye* (1964) is used by McLuhan to indicate that the use of space in Chinese painting is related to the Chinese use of intervals to get "in touch" (*Laws*, p. 43). That is, the Chinese are not interested in links and connections (linearity), but in the "resonant interval." The reason is that the Chinese ideogram "is an inclusive *gestalt*, not an analytic dissociation of senses and functions like phonetic writing" (McLuhan, 1964b, p. 84).

W. Scott Morton (1980) notes that the main materials of traditional Chinese painting were ink and watercolors, and paper and silk, not oil and canvas. A basic difference is therefore already present in the materials. An examination of the use of watercolor by a Western painter such as Andrew Wyeth (see Corn, 1973) reveals the same delicacy of line and a similar use of "blank" space. As Morton wrote, "The principle of the positive value of emptiness emerges in painting in the artist's creative use of space. It would be idle to pretend that this idea exists only in China, for all great artists everywhere employ it instinctively in composition" (1980, p. 109).

In contrast to Chiang Yee's emphasis on spaces, John Hay (1974) illustrated other aspects. "The linear quality of Chinese art," Hay wrote, "has often been noted" (1974, p. 12). He continued:

There is in Chinese painting a tradition of narrative depiction with an exactitude of detail that can rival the most documentary Western art, but it is little known in the West. . . . [T]he ability of the Chinese brush in describing the minute details of everyday life may well be unexpected. (Hay, 1974, p. 15)

The Whorfian Link

McLuhan saw oral or preliterate cultures as having the same worldview or perceptual bias as Chinese culture. "Tribal cultures cannot entertain the possibility of the individual or of the separate citizen" (McLuhan, 1964b, p. 84), because "only alphabetic cultures have ever mastered connected lineal sequences as pervasive forms of psychic and social organization" (p. 85). There is, of course, a radical difference between the Chinese, with an elaborate *written* language, and any preliterate people; but McLuhan's hypothesis was that not only certain concepts (individualism, universal harmony) are "caused" by language (oral or script), but also certain cognitive constructs: connected linear sequences in alphabetic cultures; resonant intervals in nonalphabetic cultures. This is the hypothesis of Benjamin Lee Whorf (1956). As George Miller and David McNeill state in their review of research on this hypothesis, "Cognition in general is thus held to be patterned after language" (1969, p. 733). This was exactly the McLuhan position. Philip Marchand tells us how compatible McLuhan found the Whorfian thesis "that language shapes the way we experience the world" (1989, p. 117), since it seemed to correspond to the ideas of I. A. Richards under whom McLuhan had studied at Cambridge. Miller and McNeill found no support for McLuhan's version of Whorf's theory. Thomas Steinfatt (1989) summarized what was currently known about Whorf's linguistic hypothesis, including many studies from areas not previously discussed as studies of linguistic relativity, such as "language acquisition, bidialectism, bilingualism, aphasia, and deafness" (1989, p. 35). Steinfatt noted that studies analyzing Jean Piaget's work confirmed the view that "language is not the source of logic but rather is structured by it" (p. 37).

In a section on Chinese–English studies, Steinfatt referred to the work of Alfred Bloom (1981), who claimed that the Chinese language does not contain a counterfactual structure (e.g., 'if there were no alphabet, no one could think sequentially'). The suggestion made is that, without being able to state conditions contrary to the facts, the Chinese would have found scientific thought difficult if not impossible. Steinfatt reports a study that failed "to replicate Bloom's finding of Chinese speakers' failure to understand counterfactual reasoning" (1989, p. 57); and A. C. Graham (1989) gave examples of counterfactuals used by Confucius, and noted that Bloom's case was based on modern—not classical—Chinese.

In brief, Steinfatt came to the following conclusions:

(1) The results with the deaf provide strong evidence that logical operations do not suffer from a lack of language. The evidence from the deaf seems so compelling that we can essentially dismiss the LR–LO (Linguistic Relativity—Logical Operations) hypothesis. . . .

(2) Work with the deaf again suggests rather strongly that no LR–GCS (Linguistic Relativity–General Cognitive Structure) effect can be ascribed to language. . . .

(3) If by linguistic relativity we mean that someone thinking in a particular language is not used to and does not *normally* think or use language in a particular fashion, . . . Bloom's experiments illustrate this result. But if we mean that language influences thought to the extent that one *cannot* think . . . , say, counterfactually, because of a deficit provided by a native language, then we find no evidence for the position in Bloom's results. (Steinfatt, 1989, pp. 60, 61, 62–63)

In their "Introduction to Language, Culture and Thinking" of the collected volume *Thinking* (1977), P. N. Johnson-Laird and P. C. Wason provide support from a broader, cognitive point of view: "It is difficult to resist the conclusion that language is more likely to reflect an individual's attitude to life (and schooling) perhaps absorbed from others of the same social class, than to mould such attitudes" (p. 445). Youichi Ito said the same thing: "While human psychology is basically the same all over the world, culture affects psychology and cultural differences cause different individual, particularly social, differences" (1989, p. 173).

Neither the Whorfian nor the McLuhan thesis of language holds in the face of years of testing. The medium (language and scripts) is not the message.

On this issue it is interesting to read *The Alphabet and the Brain: The*

Lateralization of Writing by Derrick de Kerckhove and Charles J. Lumsden (1988). The work is a collection of papers each of which addressed a facet of the McLuhan hypothesis of the effect of writing on the brain. Here was the search for experimental proof wanted by William Kuhns (1989). In their general conclusion, de Kerckhove and Lumsden wrote, "There are good reasons to believe that there are causal relationships between the nature of writing systems and specific cultural and cognitive consequences, but we cannot hope to answer this question completely at the level of neuropsychology right now" (1988, p. 443). This wistful hope was completely negated in two of the papers in the book, however. Insup Taylor observed that "a logography is not as pictorial as has been claimed, nor is an alphabet completely logical" (1988, p. 202), and that, "in processing textual materials, the East and West do not differ greatly" (p. 227). Ovid J. L. Tzeng and Daisy L. Hung, for their part, presented data that showed "unequivocal evidence against any suggestion that Chinese logographs are processed in the right hemisphere" p. 285), nor had they seen "any convincing evidence to suggest a modification of cerebral organization due to such orthographic variations" (p. 286). A clearer refutation of the message would be hard to find.

There Is a Difference

None of this is meant to say that there is not a difference in sensibility between Chinese and Western cultures. There is, after all, a difference between English and French cultures and between European and American cultures. These differences develop out of geographical and historical situations, and one generation teaches the next; the vocabulary and structure of languages is a creation of these phenomena. So the impact on China of the Japanese invasion of 1894–95 "awakened many Chinese to the necessity of fundamental changes in thought," and "one of the foremost attacks on the old order was the call for a vernacular language and literature" (Kwok, 1965, pp. 5–6). Part of this reform was "to enable the Chinese language to absorb modern scientific terminology" (p. 8). This was not a change to the alphabet, but a refining of the traditional ideogram. The language was adjusted to the expression of new ideas. This conforms with the research results negating Whorfian linguistic relativity.

Indeed, without that evidence, the following sentence from Joseph Needham's *Time and Eastern Man* (1965), taken out of context, could be interpreted as a direct result of the gestalt of the ideogram: "Essentially the Chinese method was analogical—like causes bring like effects, as it was then so it is now, and so it will be forever" (p. 16). This was the conclusion to a discussion of why the study of history helped to inhibit the growth of the sciences of nature. As Needham said, some have "gone so far as to urge that the pre-eminence of history is almost alone sufficient to account for the failure of Chinese culture to develop systematic logic on Aristotelian and scholastic lines out of the brilliant beginnings of the Mohist and Logicians" (p. 15). Just as it was possible to find a better reason for T. S. Eliot's perception of simultaneity (because the evidence was *there*), so Needham gives a better reason for the Chinese way of thinking about the world.

The main cause of the difference, according to Joseph Needham, one of the world's foremost scholars of Chinese civilization, is the contrasting social conditions of the ancient philosophers of China and Greece, pointing "especially to the proto-feudal bureaucratic character of the one and the city-state democracy of the other" (Needham, 1965, p. 15). In Greece, it was possible to argue a point in the assembly, equal to equal, where "every man could argue back." The Chinese philosophers, on the other hand, frequented the courts of feudal princes and could not discuss ideas with equals.

The democratic method of logical argumentation was not feasible in discussions with an absolute ruler, but an entirely different method, the citation of historical examples, could make a great impression. Thus it was that proof by historical examples prevailed very early in Chinese history over proof by logical argument. (Needham, 1965, p. 15)

It is interesting that Joel Mokyr (1990), in searching for an answer to the question why China had not built on its early technological inventiveness, could only agree with Needham.

In the 1961 Oxford Symposium on the History of Science, Needham (1963), whose monumental *Science and Civilization in China* (1954–86) was still in progress, addressed directly the relationship of the ideographic script to Chinese scientific development. Here again, it would be possible to *correlate* the invention of the printing press to the rise of modern science, and from there to perceive the alphabet as cause. Here is what Needham said:

Whatever the individual prepossessions of Western historians of science, all are necessitated to admit that from the fifteenth century A.D. onwards a complex of changes occurred; the Renaissance cannot be thought of without the Reformation, the Reformation cannot be thought of without the rise of modern science, and none of them can be thought of without the rise of capitalism, capitalist society and the decline and the disappearance of feudalism. We seem to be in the presence of an organic whole, a packet of change, the analysis of which has hardly yet begun. (Needham, 1963, p. 139)

Nothing like this happened in China. It remained a feudal society, or a protofeudal one, until the twentieth century. In religion, "harmonious

cooperation of all beings" arose not from the orders of a superior authority (a God) prescribing laws and rules of behavior, but "from the
fact that they were all parts in a hierarchy of wholes forming a cosmic
and organic pattern" (Needham, 1963, p. 136). The Chinese position
was more human and ethical in content and did not relate to nonhu-
man—that is, supernatural—nature. The conception of laws "ordained
from the beginning by a celestial law-giver from non-human nature"
never developed; hence, "the conclusion did not follow that other lesser
rational beings could decipher or reformulate the laws of a great rational
Super-Being if they used the methods of observation, experiment, hypothesis and mathematical reasoning" (p. 136).

McLuhan could have argued that this all came about because of the
nonalphabetic nature of the Chinese language, which prevented its users
from perceiving the world as fragmented, and from formulating abstract
concepts. Needham spoke to this: "There is a commonly received idea
that the ideographic language was a powerful inhibitory factor to the
development of modern science in China. We believe, however, that
this influence is grossly over-rated" (1963, p. 137). He noted that the
Chinese language of the present day is "no impediment" to science,
having undergone fifty years of work by the National Institute of Compilation and Translation to define technical terms for modern usage—
but still in ideographic form.

This is not to say that language was not a factor. Written Chinese was
essentially literary and metaphorical in nature, and "was very different
from vulgar parlance and technical language, and thus inventors were
able to make their discoveries known only with difficulty" (Chu-Ming,
1961, p. 166). It was not a matter of being either ideograph or alphabet.

One of the difficulties in trying to understand a foreign culture, or
any new complexity, is to avoid reducing the "phenomenon" to a simple
summary statement that is used to "get a handle" on it. McLuhan was
prone to do this, dealing as he was with all history and all cultures,
more often in conversation and interviews where the fast phrase is
appropriate. The Chinese essence (the Eastern philosophy) is one phenomenon that most Westerners reduce to 'the harmony of all things and
familial reverence.' Particularly in the 1960s was this so, with the popularity of such movements as transcendental meditation and various
swamis and gurus selling touchy-feely cures for the Western disease of
commercialism and technological determinism. However, the East is not
quite as unified as this reduction leads one to believe. James Cahill said
in his Charles Eliot Norton lectures at Harvard in 1979 that, long before
the Ming dynasty ended in 1644, the Confucian ideal of service to state
and society "could no longer hold" (1982, p. 1). There was widespread
questioning of the whole social structure: "Individualistic philosophies
such as those of Li Ch'ih and the 'Wild Ch'an' adherents, which aimed

at personal polarization rather than at social harmony, coexisted with movements that urged a return to Confucian basics and government reform" (p. 2). At this point the country was invaded by foreigners— the Manchu—whose dynasty lasted from 1644 to 1912. That ended the questioning. Cahill noted the tendency of people to find in Chinese painting, as a whole, a singleness of purpose and method that it never had.

Some observations about the whole tradition were made long ago and have been regularly repeated ever since: Chinese painting is concerned with revealing universal aspects of nature, not transient phenomena; it aims at representing inner essences, not outer forms; it is fundamentally an art of line and distinct brushstrokes; it is much given, especially in its later phases, to copying or imitating the past; it places little premium on originality; and so forth. Each of these statements contains some measure of truth, but each is of the same degree and order of truth as the counterobservations made by Chinese or sinophile writers about European painting: that it reflects the materialistic character of Western civilization, that it is obsessed with the human figure, that it has left largely unexploited the expressive capacity of sensitive brushwork. People who might be nettled by simplistic statements of that kind have been strangely re- ceptive to similarly sweeping ones about Chinese painting and to writers who offer to teach us about its principles, its Tao, or its mystic essence. (Cahill, 1982, pp. 2–3)

2

The McLuhan Approach to Evidence

THE CASE OF THE TWO BRAIN HEMISPHERES

The second chapter of McLuhan's *Laws of Media* is called "Culture and Communication: The Two Hemispheres." Brain hemisphericity is used as if it were completely controlled by cultural phenomena. The two halves of the brain are treated as if they were separate entities, visual space being the "result" of the dominant left hemisphere that is "restricted" to cultures with a phonetic alphabet. Immersion in this alphabet suppresses the right hemisphere (p. 69).

It is my intention to examine the hemisphere literature McLuhan used as evidence to support his idea of a cultural visual/acoustic "space" dichotomy, and then to look at other literature on the two brain hemispheres that was available prior to the publication of *Laws of Media*.

The first source cited was an article by Robert J. Trotter (1976), senior editor of *Science News* and listed on the masthead as responsible for "behavioral sciences." Trotter summarized brain research from Paul Broca to Roger Wolcott Sperry in a few paragraphs, then described an anthropological study of the Inuit by Solomon H. Katz (1975). The conclusion was that the Inuit are basically 'right-brained' in their cognitive abilities, their art, and in the structure of their language. This conclusion fitted well with McLuhan's thesis that literate cultures with a phonetic alphabet are left-brained.

Trotter's article had a chart that listed several functions of the brain and associated them with the left and right hemispheres. Thus the left hemisphere functions included speech, verbal, logical, linear, analytic, reading, writing; the right hemisphere list included spatial, musical, artistic, creative, intuitive, simultaneous, and synthetic. Looking at Trotter's chart, McLuhan saw that the main feature of the left hemisphere— linearity—was the same as the main feature of visual space. He therefore called it the "visual (quantitative) side" of the brain. The main features of the right hemisphere were simultaneous, holistic, and synthetic, or the "acoustic (qualitative) side" (*Laws*, p. 69).

Trotter had taken his brain functions from Katz (1975), who culled them from the early split-brain studies of Roger Wolcott Sperry, Michael Gazzaniga, and Joseph Bogen, and from a survey of cultural beliefs about the left and right sides of the body found in the literature of anthropology. Katz was a professor of physical anthropology at the University of Pennsylvania and medical scientist at Eastern Pennsylvania Psychiatric Clinic. The literature of psychiatry and psychotherapy has recorded lists of body characteristics for many years, both left and right sides, top and bottom halves, and front and back. Edward L. Smith (1985), for example, refers to the meanings of the left side, controlled by the right hemisphere, as including orientation in space, integrative cognitive style, spatial relationships, musical perception. The meanings of the right side of the body, controlled by the left hemisphere, include the logical, analytic thinking, verbal and mathematical abilities, speech and writing. Quite clearly, these are the same as those in Trotter's list.

Trotter said that handedness had been found to be a fairly reliable sign of "hemisphere activation" (1976, p. 219). However, Janet Dunaif-Hattis found that "the presence or absence of handedness is not necessarily an indication of a similar pattern of cognitive asymmetries" (1984, p. 12). Dunaif-Hattis is careful to distinguish between cognitive and physiological asymmetries. Information about handedness in the investigation of brain lateralization must be used with restraint.

Nevertheless, let's see what Trotter did with handedness as he understood it—and as McLuhan read it. Because most people are right handed—that is, 'left brained'—and "because the speech centers are almost always located in the left hemisphere, that hemisphere has usually been considered 'dominant' " (Trotter, 1976, p. 219). After noting that all the Inuit carvers studied were right handed (p. 220), Trotter ignored that 'fact' (if right handed, then the left brain is dominant) and reported Katz's description of the work of the left hand in cradling the piece being carved as proof that the Inuit were right brain dominant. That is, the left hand held the piece, while the right hand did the work.

Criticisms of Trotter's article appeared in the letters column of *Science News* on May 8, 1976, one of them calling our attention to "self-fulfilling hemisphere myths." Indeed, Katz had constructed his brain function lists before studying the Inuit, and Trotter pointed out what Katz had admitted: that the lists were "only intuitive at present" (1976, p. 220).

Nevertheless, Trotter and McLuhan accepted the dichotomy of functions as scientific facts.

Since Trotter's article, but prior to the publication of *Laws*, there has been enough evidence in the literature that the dichotomy between the hemispheres is more a "matter of degree than a difference in kind" (Bradshaw and Nettleton, 1983, p. 264) to give the serious scientist pause. Alan Beaton concurred, finding that "it has not been shown, for example, that one hemisphere is totally incapable of carrying out functions normally ascribed to its partner" (1985, p. 286). Chris Code, more recently, confirmed that position: "We no longer believe that 'language' is produced and comprehended by one or two discretely localized centres or mechanisms of the left hemisphere" (1987, p. 168). Alan Beaton's closing words are salutary:

Perhaps the search for a dichotomy of function between left and right hemispheres is bound to fail. There is, after all, no reason *why* the brain should have evolved so conveniently. Certainly, many of the phenomena of everyday life cannot be described as *either* analytic *or* holistic, temporal *or* spatial or whatever. (Beaton, 1985, pp. 287–88)

We will need to keep this in mind, for the literature reviewed below assumes the dichotomy or does not always make Beaton's qualification, so appealing is it to speak of the two halves of the brain as if, in fact, they were two separate brains altogether.

Split-brain Research

In a footnote (*Laws*, p. 69), McLuhan referred to Michael S. Gazzaniga's 1977 review of split-brain research. Tests of patients after commissurotomy (the surgical procedure to "split" the two halves of the brain) indicated a dichotomy of abilities of the two hemispheres.

The review literature is extremely doubtful about the validity of these results and the relevance of split-brain studies to normal brains. Beaton provided this caution:

It is also clear that the left and right hemispheres of the split-brain patient differ to some extent in the functions that they each carry out. However, every patient who has undergone total commissurotomy has previously suffered from long-standing epilepsy. This may have caused some cerebral re-organization of function. Results obtained from split-brain patients, therefore, may not apply to normal individuals with an intact corpus callosum. (Beaton, 1985, p. 61)

The corpus callosum is a bundle of nerve fibers linking the two halves of the brain.

The surgery itself also does damage to the brain. Janice Millar and Harry Whitaker gave the following description.

The split-brain operation is a neurosurgical procedure designed to limit the spread of epileptic seizures across the corpus callosum, the major (but not only) connection between the Left and Right hemispheres. In the operation, the skull is opened, one hemisphere, usually the nondominant, is pulled aside to expose the corpus callosum; a large number of arteries and veins which run between the two hemispheres are coagulated; and the corpus callosum (and occasionally one or more other interhemispheric commissures) is divided almost totally. The operation itself causes some brain damage, inevitably. Pulling aside one hemisphere (retraction) bruises the hemisphere along its mesial (inside, or middle) surface; coagulating the bridging arteries and veins causes the death of the tissue supplied by those arteries and veins. Presumably, retrograde axonal degeneration of the callosal fibres causes some changes in both the Left and Right hemispheres. However, these are not the significant extracallosal brain damage. The lesions responsible for the epilepsy are the principle extracallosal brain damage. (Millar and Whitaker, 1983, pp. 102–3)

It is, then, not surprising to read Code's more recent conclusion:

Despite, or maybe because of, the impact of the commissurotomy findings, split-brain research has come in for some fierce criticism in more recent years. It should be recalled that the operation has been carried out on a very few individuals and the entire but extensive commissurotomy literature is based on a mere handful of cases. . . . The major criticism of the research is that the findings must at least be reviewed with considerable reservation or even completely discounted, on the grounds that the data give a false impression of the hemisphere capabilities of the normal brain. (Code, 1987, p. 10)

Even at that, the Gazzaniga article quoted by McLuhan was not as convincing about the strict dichotomy of functions as we were led to believe. Gazzaniga warned there was some evidence that hinted at a redundancy—"a redundancy which suggests that all language and all spatial functions are not strictly and exclusively lateralized to the respective left and right hemispheres" (1977, p. 94).

More support for the dichotomous functioning of the brain was mustered by McLuhan from the work of Joseph Bogen. McLuhan cited Bogen's speculative paper "Some Educational Implications of Hemispheric Specialization" (1977). Bogen had been involved in studying split-brain patients, and it is edifying to read the reports. In one such report, Bogen and his coauthors (1972) describe the tests they used to investigate the functioning of the two hemispheres of split-brain patients. The paper is full of qualifications. For example, they concluded, "This leads to the concept of 'hemisphericity,' i.e. a tendency for a person to rely more on one hemisphere than the other. If such 'hemisphericity' exists, it may well reflect influences of early cultural exposure" (Bogen et al., 1972, p. 50). The words *cultural exposure* would have excited McLuhan, because it is exactly what he would have said himself. But note the hesitancy of the words *if* it exists and *it may well*. There is no scientific fact here.

One of Bogen's tests—the Street test—involved recognition of pictures from more and less recognizable patterns. The following quotation qualified the results significantly.

For solving the Street test, there are three possible cerebral loci: (1) the left hemisphere solves the problem by itself, then answers. Or (2) the right hemisphere solves the problem and then serves up the answer for the left hemisphere to express. Or (3) the two hemispheres work together, transcommissurally, toward a solution which is eventually uttered by the left hemisphere. In patients with cerebral commissurotomy, processes (2) and (3) can contribute very little whereas in the intact person one or the other is most important. *The data presented further on cannot distinguish between (2) and (3).* (Bogen et al., 1972, p. 51, fn., emphasis added)

That is, in normal brains, you can't tell which side is doing what. I imagine that is why Bogen later hedged his program for educational curricula to address 'right brain' learning, by saying he wasn't sure about the nature of hemisphericity but, "for now, I would offer the short answer: assuming two types of intelligence, rather than some larger number, not only appeals for reasons of simplicity, but it has the very important advantage of conforming with the physiology of the brain" (1977, p. 137). By his own evidence, it only conforms with the physiology of the brain that has been split.

Nor can we assume two types of intelligence when we have J. P. Guilford's work providing evidence for "some 81 intellectual abilities" and "the prospect is for more than the 120 abilities originally hypothesized" (1967, p. 465). Indeed, without any reference to the underlying physiology, or the effects of visual or acoustic space, Guilford came to the same conclusion as Bogen and McLuhan about the desirability of engaging all facets of the thinking process in educational programs. After noting that the Stanford-Binet intelligence tests placed too much emphasis on cognitive abilities and not enough on divergent production and classes and transformation, Guilford concluded:

Whereas much teaching effort is directed at the formation of concepts, which is weighted toward the cognition of semantic units, considerably more is needed in the exercise of other products: classes, relations, systems, transformation, and implications. It is involvement with the latter that gives significance and meaning to units of information and that makes information useful. (Guilford, 1967, p. 476)

It is these products, identified after years of painstaking research, that can be matched to the functions of the right hemisphere: spatial, synthetic, gestalt, holistic, and simultaneous expression.

It is the "appealing" nature of hemisphericity that attracts people, and its simplicity, which reduces what is so complex we don't understand it to a duality that can be encompassed in catchy phrases. Julian Jaynes (1977) did the same sort of thing, but had no compunction about saying his work was purely speculative. Quoting Jaynes to support anything amounts to basing one's structure on mist. Jaynes relied on Bogen and Gazzaniga and their work with split-brain patients. He also referred to Wilder Penfield's stimulation of specific areas of the brain by electrodes. Beaton commented on Penfield's cautionary note that the effects of cortical stimulation are not consistent since electrical interference in a given area is only effective about 50 percent of the time (Beaton, 1985, p. 114).

Jaynes himself, in a footnote, disqualified Penfield's data by stating that, while he was following Penfield as the "traditional" authority, "some of it is out of date in the present explosion of knowledge in this area" (Jaynes, 1977, p. 101).

Betty Edwards, author of the popular *Drawing on the Right Side of the Brain* (1979), recognized the altered knowledge about the split brain and quickly changed from a physiological 'L-mode' and 'R-mode' to the use of those terms to designate styles of thinking.

The most positive statement about hemisphericity among the rigorous scientific researchers is probably this summary by Code:

We must start by saying that a comprehensive and integrated theory of the right hemisphere in communication is not possible at this stage in our knowledge. Nonetheless, as we have seen, researchers have proposed models to account for certain aspects of communication apparently mediated with right hemisphere involvement, although many are unhappy with attempts to subsume hemispheric differences in terms of opposing modes of processing. Whether the currently pursued complementary specialization model, and its main expression the analytic-holistic dichotomy, will continue to produce worthwhile research questions remains to be seen. Certainly, the notion that a cognitive balance is achieved by two fundamentally distinct methods of processing information is appealing. It is rooted in a long cultural, spiritual and scientific history, and may be the highest known human expression of asymmetry that exists in nature. (Code, 1987, p. 167)

And maybe not.

Animal Brain Asymmetry

Using George Steiner's *After Babel* (1975) as a source, McLuhan came to conclusions about the origins of speech and hemisphericity. The relevant quotation from Steiner was this:

In an estimated 97 per cent of human adults language is controlled by the left hemisphere of the brain. The difference shows up in the anatomy of the upper surface of the temporal lobe (in 65 per cent of cases studied, the *planum temporale* on the left side of the brain was one-third longer than on the right). This asymmetry, which seems to be genetically determined, is dramatized by the fact that the great majority of human beings are right-handed. Evidence for this goes back to the earliest stone tools. No such cerebral unbalance has been found in primates or any other animal species. (Steiner, 1975, pp. 280–81, quoted in *Laws* at p. 119, where a footnote informs us that Steiner's sources were Norman Geschwind and Walter Levitsky, 1968, and Geschwind, 1972)

Not quoted in *Laws* is what follows directly after in Steiner, which warns us that we are not being given scientific facts but speculation.

Unlike animal species we are out of balance with and in the world. Speech is the consequence and maintainer of this disequilibrium. Interpretation (translation [the subject of Steiner's book]) keeps the pressures of inventive excess from overwhelming and randomizing the medium. It limits the play of private intention, of plurality in meaning, at least at a rough and ready level of functional consensus. In an ambiguity which is at one level ontological and at another ironic, idiomatic level, political or social, we speak left and act right. Translation mediates: it constrains the constant drive to dispersion. But this too, of course, is *conjecture*. (Steiner, 1975, pp. 281–82, emphasis added)

For Steiner, it is translation that saves us from the domination of one half of the brain; for McLuhan, it is the media of communication that push us either left or right.

McLuhan used Steiner's statements about animals to say that the imbalance or asymmetry in the human brain is related to or results in speech (*Laws*, p. 119). This strongly reflects Steiner's conjecture that "speech is the consequence" of the imbalance. What is the evidence regarding asymmetry in animal brains?

John Bradshaw and Norman Nettleton described the "great similarity between humans and certain species of bird—the left-brain control of song (in birds) and speech (in humans)" (1983, p. 14). They concluded that

apes alone show similar (though smaller) left–right morphological asymmetries of the brain to humans in the peri-Sylvian regions, which are speech-related in humans. It is uncertain, however, to what extent this could be related to communication, unless apes are simply preadapted for the evolutionary development of lateralized control systems. (Bradshaw and Nettleton, 1983, p. 20)

Dunaif-Hattis presented considerable data on animal asymmetry (1984, pp. 101–16). This evidence supports Steiner's statement, somehow missed by McLuhan, that the asymmetry is "genetically determined," not culturally determined. Thus the argument in *Laws* that brain asymmetry is strongly related to the origin of speech directly contradicts McLuhan's basic theory that the use of the left or right 'brains' is caused by "environmental factors" (*Laws*, p. 72).

Insecurity of Hemisphere Research Generally

In their discussion of asymmetries in species other than humans, Bradshaw and Nettleton cautioned that "a *structural asymmetry* does not necessarily imply a *functional asymmetry*" (1983, p. 14). Dunaif-Hattis quoted one study that reported as follows:

Although there may be an apparent directional correlation between anatomic asymmetry and functional asymmetry, it does not prove that the anatomic asymmetry is a substrate for the functional asymmetry, or that the functional asymmetry is a manifestation of the anatomic asymmetry. In fact, the statistical distributions of each asymmetry are sufficiently disparate to cause concern for such interpretation. (from Dunaif-Hattis, 1984, p. 18)

Beaton, in his comprehensive review of the literature, also raised a cautionary note about ascribing specific functions to the left and right hemispheres, particularly 'propositional' and 'appositional' (Bogen's terms; see Bogen, 1977), verbal versus nonverbal, linguistic versus spatial, analytic versus holistic, and rational versus intuitive (1985, p. 285).

Bradshaw and Nettleton (1983) also noted problems of interpretation. While the research findings indicated a considerable number of left–right morphological asymmetries, particularly in language-related areas of the cortex, it was also clear that "these differences are often small, apparent only in reasonably large samples, and continuously distributed" (Bradshaw and Nettleton, 1983, p. 27). That is, there is not an all or none situation as is the case for the spleen or liver being on one side of the body. Beaton, among his many other comments on hemisphere research methodological difficulties, said of the small differences mentioned above that "the point is that if a variable is continuously distributed, the choice of a cut-off criterion for classifying different groups of subjects (say into left or mixed handers) is entirely arbitrary" (1985, p. 9).

Bradshaw and Nettleton (1983) and Beaton (1985) both commented on the difficulties of measuring parts of the brain. Beaton's description gives a hint of the complications.

The posterior extent of the planum temporale has usually been determined by inserting a knife blade into the Sylvian fissure and advancing it until the posterior wall is reached. However, Rubens, Mahowald and Hutton . . . found that in 25 of 36 brains the Sylvian fissure on the right side angulated more sharply upward than on the left. Consequently, the "posterior wall" of the Sylvian fissure may not represent the true termination of this fissure. Since it is not yet known how often the auditory association area is limited in its posterior extent by this angulation, gross measures of anatomical asymmetry may not represent a valid index of asymmetry of auditory association cortex. (Beaton, 1985, pp. 147–48)

Psychological testing seems even less reliable than physical measurements. Recall the above-quoted footnote from Bogen and coauthors (1972) about the inability of the picture identification tests to distinguish which side of the brain was doing the work when the halves were intact. Beaton was unequivocal in his judgment that it is impossible to specify accurately the part of the brain where "neural events" take place between stimulus and response (1985, p. 94).

Bradshaw and Nettleton were equally cautious about clinical tests.

Clinical studies of lateralized brain function, though long established, are beset by many problems of interpretation. The clinician has little control over his or her source material, the exact limits of brain injuries may be unclear, and while lesions may be localizable, the same cannot always be said of symptoms. Chains of facilitation and inhibition may cause a quite distant area to appear to mediate a particular function when in fact it plays only a minor or indirect role. Individual differences in brain function, nature of the disease, age, sex, educational attainment, and even motivation can all mask or accentuate the apparent consequences of brain injury. Since different disabilities are disabling for different vocations, not everyone is equally likely to seek treatment for otherwise comparable clinical conditions. Even publication rates are biased toward the more frequent reporting of the less common syndromes, leading to a possible false impression of prevalence of certain conditions. (Bradshaw and Nettleton, 1983, p. 51)

With these caveats in mind, and realizing that we are therefore dealing with interpretation rather than empirically incontrovertible fact, it is the very careless scholar who would refer to brain hemisphericity in absolutist terms.

Faces

McLuhan thought the " 'acoustic' power of simultaneous comprehension" enabled the right hemisphere to recognize faces (*Laws*, p. 70). Given the discussion of the problems inherent in hemisphericity research, what evidence is there that faces as "wholes" are not recognized by the left side of the brain? Bradshaw and Nettleton find none: "Face recognition does not seem to be an exclusively right hemisphere function, despite the fact that faces are typically recognized by global, holistic, or relational rather than by piecemeal processes" (1983, p. 53).

Eleanor Gibson has, perhaps, the explanation: "Development seems to proceed from simple contours to differentiated features to structured relations or patterns to unique patterns of individual faces, and finally to higher order properties invariant over different individual faces" (1969, p. 347). In other words, it is not one or the other side of the brain at work, but the whole brain that is putting the pieces together, learning to recognize—over time and with practice.

Concluding Remarks on Brain Hemisphere Research

What more needs to be said about the ability of researchers to measure the connection between the brain hemispheres and cognitive skills? Julie Dumbrower and coauthors (1981) conducted an elaborate test to "determine the construct validity of measures hypothesized to represent an orientation to Right, Left, or integrated hemispheric brain function" among primary school children. Their conclusion was as follows:

Factor analyses of correlation matrices for selected pretest and for selected post-test scores in general did not lend support for the two hypotheses (1) that measures intended to represent an RH [right hemisphere] orientation would define a separate factor dimension and (2) that measures designed to reflect an LH [left hemisphere] orientation would describe a second dimension essentially independent of the first. Thus, construct validity of measures hypothesized to portray an RH or LH orientation in brain function could not be demonstrated with a high degree of confidence for the samples studied. (Dumbrower et al., 1981, p. 1192)

Six years later, writing in the *Journal of Learning Disabilities*, Merrill Hiscock and Marcel Kinsbourne confirmed these results in the following comment on the popular belief in the specialization of the hemispheres.

Insofar as the normal brain is characterized by functional differentiation of the cerebral hemispheres, it is not unreasonable to suspect that at least some learning disorders are associated with deviation from the usual pattern of hemispheric specialization. Nonetheless, the available data generally have failed to confirm this suspicion . . . [and thus] left and right hemispheric cognitive styles are metaphors without a proven neurological basis. (Hiscock and Kinsbourne, 1987, p. 140)

There seems little doubt that human brain asymmetry and a graded functional lateralization constitute part of the natural structure of the body. Colwyn Trevarthen reported that:

Psychological tests of young babies show that perceptual categorization of speech sounds into entities that correspond with consonants and syllables in the production of mature speakers occurs very early in infancy, probably from birth.

... These findings support the view that complex perceptual mechanisms specialized to regulate speech are innate in man and function at some level in infancy. (Trevarthen, 1983, p. 64)

Jerre Levy acknowledged that the majority of primitive humans as far back as Australopithecus had an enlarged parieto occipital region on the left side and that evidence of weapon use indicates most were right handed (1974, p. 121). Bradshaw and Nettleton also referred to studies finding that paleolithic tools and weapons were made by and for the right hand (1983, p. 190). Norman Geschwind (1972), footnoted in *Laws* (p. 119) as a citation from Steiner (1975), also made the point that "it seems likely that the asymmetries of the brain are genetically determined"(Geschwind, 1972, p. 83).

Michael C. Corballis gave a summary of the issue.

For centuries, there has been dispute over whether human laterality, and in particular human handedness, is fundamentally biological or whether it is shaped by culture. At this particular point in history, it seems inescapable that the predominant pattern of right-handedness and left-hemispheric specialization for linguistic and praxic skills is essentially biological and programmed into the structure of the nervous system. This pattern appears to be universal among human beings of all cultures, in all parts of the globe, through recorded history, and possibly extending back in prehistory to our hominid ancestors of perhaps 2 or 3 million years ago. Precursors to human laterality can be detected in newborn infants, well before environmental or cultural influences could plausibly be thought to exert any systematic bias. In the normal course of events, and among the majority of people, environment or culture play only a minor role in modifying or reinforcing this biological disposition to lateralization. (Corballis, 1983, p. 197)

In an article that was the basis for the second chapter of *Laws of Media*, McLuhan wrote, "The dominance of either left or right hemisphere is largely dependent upon environmental factors" (1978, p. 55)—a statement repeated in *Laws* (p. 72). Based on the evidence, that statement is simply not valid. It might be that different cultures can be related to different ways of thinking about the world and that these ways of thinking can be categorized by the dichotomies listed earlier, but these ways of thinking are variations on a common genetic foundation of brain structure and function that cannot be altered in any fundamental way by environmental influences. Nonetheless, when we come down from generalities and averages to the level of the individual person, some genetic factors can be overcome by willpower. Winston Churchill's battle with his endomorphic nature is only one well-known instance (Manchester, 1988). The *media* cannot alter biology.

The explanatory simplicity that was the result of split-brain research had great appeal. Associating styles of thinking with the functions of the left and right hemispheres had the air and feel of secure scientific knowledge. After all, this was a physical thing, and things can be grasped much more easily than psychological discriminations—at least the surface of things. But neither the brain nor human life is simple. To accept a simplistic approach to culture is to lose contact with it. Culture is as complex as anything in human experience and cannot be reduced to left/right brain functions or visual/acoustic space characteristics.

In any case, visual/acoustic space characteristics do not need reference to hemisphericity to be interesting and enlightening avenues of discovering something about the human condition. Rather than adopting the popular science view of brain lateralization, McLuhan would have been wiser to eschew any reference to it as a scientific foundation for his theories. In fact, in one instance, McLuhan did recognize that the hemispheres are not really separate and that Orientals are not really right-brained.

But no matter how extreme the dominance of either hemisphere in a particular culture, there is always some degree of interplay, thanks to the *corpus callosum*, that part of the nervous system which bridges the hemispheres. Even the Chinese with their traditionally monopolistic cultivation of the right hemisphere which invests every aspect of their lives, their language, and their writing with artistic delicacy—even the Chinese exert much left-hemisphere stress through their practicality and their concern with moral wisdom. (*Laws*, p. 176)

THE CASE OF TELEVISION AND DYSLEXIA

With the clarification of the hemisphericity problem, we can look at the evidence for McLuhan's statement that dyslexia is a "direct result" of the electric media, and particularly television (*Laws*, p. 76). He also observed that 90 percent of dyslexics are males. Two things need to be said about this proclamation right away. First, no evidence is cited to support TV's role in producing dyslexia; and second, if dyslexia is a direct result of TV and other electric media, why is there such a disparity between the sexes in those who suffer from the disability? Do girls not watch TV, listen to radio, or talk on the telephone?

Corballis cited reading disability research that showed the ratio between the sexes at four to one, boys outnumbering girls (1983, p. 183). Some studies found that, while reading difficulties are more common among boys, true dyslexia may not be. There may be other factors at work that contribute to the excess number of boys with reading problems.

For instance, boys are notoriously more prone to hyperactivity than girls, and it is likely that this contributes to difficulties in learning to read in ways unconnected with dyslexia itself. Moreover, boys are more likely than girls to suffer birth complications, such as anoxia, prematurity, miscarriages, and stillbirths, which may also explain the slightly higher incidence of left-handedness among boys [who survive]. (Corballis, 1983, p. 184)

There is a tendency toward left-handedness among those with developmental dyslexia. This would indicate a 'right brain' dominance that could be evidence for McLuhan's claim. One study cited by Corballis, which charted the pedigrees of five dyslexic children, found that "among three generations of relatives, 19 out of 45 were described as left-handed or ambidextrous" (1983, p. 180). However, this study was done in 1930, so the influence of television must be discounted.

Beaton commented that there was a possible bias in the sex composition of the samples studied and that researchers often failed to mention the sex of their subjects (1985, p. 199). In any case, there was general agreement in the literature Beaton reviewed that the disability, if not caused by brain lesions, is genetic, not cultural. Beaton cited studies showing that children with developmental dyslexia tend to have a family history of backwardness in reading. He concluded that developmental dyslexia is of constitutional origin (pp. 196–97).

A comment can be made about McLuhan's source for the link between television and dyslexia. In his collected letters (Molinaro, McLuhan, and Toye, 1987), there are two letters (pp. 534, 535) that mention Dr. Arthur Hurst, O.D., with whom McLuhan had been working on the study of vision problems. Hurst (1981) then provides us with the relevant information on their work together. He referred to the split-brain literature, which he said had "conclusively shown that the human brain has two independently functioning halves" (Hurst, 1981, p. 32), and cited one 1976 study reporting that "boys specialized in the right hemisphere as early as age 6 while girls used both hemispheres to age 13" (p. 32). The implication was that if a child—more likely a boy—had a dominant right hemisphere, he might do poorly in "reading, writing, sequential ordering and complex motor functions" (p. 32). Using McLuhan as source, Hurst then speculated in this fashion:

Excessive TV viewing *may be causing* a changeover in dominance from the left to the right hemisphere. Now males are more susceptible to this change, since by age six they are well on their way, so we *may have* a ready-made answer for the male failure in the vision-reading correlations. Unfortunately, *hard evidence is lacking* and more questions than answers have been produced. (Hurst, 1981, p. 35, emphasis added)

McLuhan gave a reason for the predominance of males with dyslexia and reading disabilities in a letter to Clare Booth Luce (in Molinaro, McLuhan, and Toye, 1987, p. 534). Dyslexia is "the direct result" of watching TV because it is the "nature of the TV image to prevent motor response in the eyes." Boys are more often the "victims" because the sports they play do not need the delicate muscular coordination that is necessary for reading. The activities of girls, such as "sewing, cooking, cosmetics, etc." help develop finer eye–hand coordinations. Since the hemisphere dominance claimed by Hurst is in place by age six, it is hard to understand what children McLuhan was thinking about. Sewing, cooking, and cosmetics are not the sole activities of girls before the age of six, any more than sports are the sole activity of boys before that age. Especially since World War II, the activities of boys and girls in these early years have been pretty much the same. In any case, we need to know which boys and which girls.

There is no evidence linking television watching to dyslexia, and what *is* known about the disability points to genetic—not environmental—factors. The media are not involved.

THE CASE OF KRUGMAN'S BRAIN WAVE STUDIES

In June 1970, Herbert Krugman, a marketing researcher for the General Electric Company, sent a paper called "Electro-encephalographic Aspects of Low Involvement: Implications for the McLuhan Hypothesis" to McLuhan at the Centre for Culture and Technology in Toronto. This was a copy of a paper delivered earlier in the year at the annual conference of the American Association for Public Opinion Research, and later published in the *Journal of Advertising Research* (Krugman, 1971). I happened to be at the Centre when this paper was on the reception desk, and McLuhan—very excitedly—had his secretary make me a copy. It is this copy, with its covering letter from Krugman, that I now have before me.

Krugman's experiment involved measuring the brain waves of a twenty-two-year-old secretary as she read a magazine and then watched three different commercials showing different moods—two calm and gentle, and one "a very explosive commercial showing star baseball pitcher Bob Gibson throwing fastballs at what looks like an unbreakable sheet of glass, actually a new product called Lexan" (Krugman, 1970, p. 9). The results showed more active brain waves for reading and more passive ones for watching the TV ads—regardless of the content of the ads. As Krugman said, "that is, the basic electrical response of the brain is clearly to the media and not to content differences within the TV commercials, or to what *we* in our pre-McLuhan days would ordinarily have called the commercial message" (pp. 13–14). He then went on to discuss how these results supported McLuhan's communication theory: "Our EEG confirms McLuhan in the sense that television is not communication as we have known it. Our subject was *trying* to learn something from a print ad, but was passive about television" (p. 16).

Philip Marchand reported McLuhan's reaction to Krugman's findings.

McLuhan, of course, was delighted with Krugman's report and kept up a correspondence with him for several years afterward. He was especially grateful to Krugman for relieving him of the burden of proof for his theories.... [McLuhan's work was now] blessed, as it were, by an authentic member of the white-coated fraternity. (Marchand, 1989, pp. 229–30)

White-coated or not, there are several things we can say about Krugman's "science." First, it was a single test with a single subject. It was not a random sample from which one could derive numbers at some statistical level of confidence. Second, there are various problems with electroencephalograms, not the least being "ignorance concerning the actual relationship of the various wave types (Delta, Theta, Alpha, Beta 1, Beta 2) to actual mental events" (Code, 1987, p. 22). The problems of interpreting EEG signals associated with brain activity, Chris Code revealed, "include interference from tissue other than brain tissue surrounding the electrodes, decisions regarding the contribution of a pair of electrodes to a change in potential difference, and the major problem of underlying asymmetrics of the brain" (p. 22). That is, while the scalp where the electrodes are symmetrically applied is itself symmetrical, the brain beneath is asymmetrical, particularly in certain regions, with a resulting confusion of signals. Code concluded that the technique was not developed to the level of distinguishing "the contribution of a hemisphere in structured experimental sessions involving even relatively simple cognitive stimuli" (p. 22). And that was nearly a decade after Krugman's experiment.

Third, and completely damaging, television was not involved at all. The test room contained "drapes, a comfortable couch, magazines on a cocktail table, and a simulated TV set in the corner at a viewing distance of seven feet from the subject" (Krugman, 1970, p. 8). The simulated TV set, as Krugman explained, was a "Fairchild 400 rear projector with an 8 × 11 inch screen. A tape cartridge held three different color commercials to be run in sequence three times for a total of nine viewings" (p. 8). One must not be misled by the word *tape*. The Fairchild 400 used a cartridge that contained a 16mm loop film, not a television tape. What the secretary watched was a 16mm film on a simulated television set.

In order to understand fully the meaning of this simulation for McLuhan's basic theory, it is necessary to read McLuhan's description of the technical nature of television and why it had the impact McLuhan hypothesized. The description is from McLuhan's *Understanding Media*:

The TV image is not a *still* shot. It is not photo in any sense, but a ceaselessly forming contour of things limned by the scanning-finger. . . . The viewer of the TV mosaic unconsciously reconfigures the dots into an abstract work of art on the pattern of a Seurat or Rouault. (McLuhan, 1964b, pp. 312–13)

Whatever else one might say about Krugman's test, without those "dots," that plastic "contour," the 'message' had nothing to do with television.

In *Laws*, McLuhan referred to another Krugman presentation that showed a "predominantly right brain response to TV" (Krugman, 1978, p. 7). I do not know if Krugman received any criticism at the conference at which this paper was presented, but considering what we know about brain hemisphericity and the difficulty of distinguishing, in the whole and healthy brain, which side is doing what, one is entitled to hesitate when one reads, for example, his report of reactions to an ad using Thomas Edison: "among our cases each individual reacts to the print with one brain hemisphere, or to the character Edison with the other brain hemisphere" (p. 3). This was reaction to a "typical one hundred and twenty second Edison commercial" (p. 2). The "print" referred to is print-over on a scene in the commercial.

We are told nothing about the "cases" or how many there were. The following sentence, quoted in *Laws* (p. 71), begs analysis.

On the larger scale, the ability of respondents to show high right brain response to even familiar logos, their right brain response to stories even before the idea content has been added to them, the predominantly right brain response to TV and perhaps even to what we call print advertising—all suggest that in contrast to teaching, the unique power of the electronic media is to *shape* the content of people's imagery and in that way determine their behavior and their views. (Krugman, 1978, p. 7)

It should be explained that the words *what we call print advertising* refer to a previous page where it is explained that "what we call 'print,' or print advertising is probably not really a left brain phenomenon, since Starch norms of 50% 'noting' and 10% 'read most' for two page-four color ads—strongly suggest that what advertising people call 'print' is primarily a picture or right brain medium too" (Krugman, 1978, p. 6). (Starch norms are measures of advertising effectiveness where, for example, 'noted' is the percent of readers who remember having seen the ad in a given publication.) The conclusion cannot, in fact, refer to "the unique power of the electronic media" since the print ad is on paper. The only logical reference from the data presented would be to the unique power of pictures, whether on paper or on television. We would then get the somewhat insipid result of discovering the power of *pictures* to shape the content of people's imagery.

3

A Sampling of Other Errors

RUTH BENEDICT AND *THE BOOK OF TEA*

In the preface to *Laws*, Eric McLuhan explained that the book started as a revision of *Understanding Media* (McLuhan, 1964b), and that he and his father began to review all the criticisms of that work, including those regarding matters of fact. There was also the matter of the frustration of readers of *Understanding Media* who said, basically, that it was not a scientific work. Then, in the McLuhans' search for what made a scientific statement, they discovered the answer in Popper's *Objective Knowledge* (1972). This was Popper's principle of falsification. As I said at the beginning, it was this recognition of Popper in *Laws* that motivated my own examination of McLuhan's work. I have already presented what I consider to be its major flaws—flaws that can only be seen as undermining and dismantling the main hypothesis that 'the medium is the message.'

In this chapter, I examine other errors that can be missed by those who become hypnotized by McLuhan's rhetoric, and who do not have the opportunity to check his sources. I have discussed *The Book of Tea* (Okakura-Kakuzo, 1912) earlier. In the same vein, strangely enough, is Ruth Benedict's *The Chrysanthemum and the Sword* (1946), used by McLuhan in *Laws* (pp. 79–81). Benedict was an acclaimed anthropologist who had been asked to prepare a description of the Japanese prior to the American occupation of that country. As one reviewer wrote, however,

This meticulous anthropological study of Japanese character suffers from one grave drawback: the author has never been to Japan. As a result it has a bookish quality that puts it at a long remove from the realities of present-day Japan. This obvious limitation escapes Dr. Benedict's supposedly trained eye. In the last chapter, she writes an unhesitating paean of praise to American occupation policy.... [H]aving seen all, she has seen nothing. (Peel, 1946)

Another review unintentionally placed the book in a class with *The Book of Tea*.

The resulting picture is not the one to be seen in Japanese homes and streets and villages today; it is a picture of which one still catches a glimpse in the traditional *Kabuki* plays and of which Japanese intellectuals sometimes talk nostalgically.... [T]his list of discrepancies could easily be extended.... Miss Benedict's book must be considered to be primarily of historical interest. (Strauss, 1946)

In response, McLuhan might have asked if these reviewers knew any Japanese, as he knew William Empson had asked about Joseph Needham of Chinese (in Molinaro, McLuhan, and Toye, 1987, p. 464). Strangely, this was the only reference McLuhan made to Needham, although Needham had been publishing copiously on matters Chinese all through the 1950s.

As it is relevant to the next section, we shall indeed ask the question now: *did* Needham know any Chinese? In the preface to the first volume (1954) of *Science and Civilization in China* (Needham, 1954–86), he tells us how he learned the language and of his many travels throughout China. In a collection of essays honoring Needham, the editors Mikulás Teich and Robert Young remarked that Needham was "at home in the ideographic language of the Chinese" (1973, p. xvii). In any event, one of the coauthors of *Science and Civilization in China*—Wang Ling—was responsible, over a seven-year period, for eight out of every ten translations used in the work. *All* translations were checked by Needham and Wang Ling before being accepted.

THE MECHANICAL CLOCK

Why McLuhan ignored Needham is a mystery. Certainly the following "fact" from *Understanding Media* could have been corrected by referring to Needham's available work: "Until the coming of the missionaries in the seventeenth century, and the introduction of mechanical clocks, the Chinese and Japanese had for thousands of years measured time by graduation of incense" (McLuhan, 1964b, p. 146). Where this information came from we are not told. But Joseph Needham, Wang Ling, and Derek de Solla Price had earlier published a very detailed technical study of medieval Chinese mechanical clocks, and noted that there had been "a long tradition of astronomical clock-making in China between the seventh and fourteenth centuries A.D." (1960, p. 2)—at least six centuries before the first European mechanical clocks.

KIERKEGAARD AND THE TELEGRAPH

A similar sort of factual error is illustrated in McLuhan's statement that Soren Kierkegaard, in his *Concept of Dread* (1944; first published in 1844), alluded to the telegraph "as a sinister technology" (*Laws*, p. 44). My curiosity aroused, I read the book carefully and found two uses of the word *telegraph*. One was in the following passage:

Revelation may declare itself in words when the unfortunate man ends by intruding upon everyone his hidden secret. It may declare itself by a look, by a glance; for there is a glance of the eye by which a man involuntarily reveals what is hidden. There is an accusing glance which one almost dreads to understand: a contrite, imploring glance which hardly tempts curiosity to peer into this involuntary telegraphy. (Kierkegaard, 1944, p. 115)

In terms of its relevance to McLuhan's statement, this use of the word could as easily refer to the signaling device invented and named by Claude Chappe in France in 1792—a device consisting of upright posts with movable arms. The electric telegraph was first publicly discussed by Don Francisco Salva at the Royal Academy of Sciences in Barcelona in 1797 (according to the *Oxford English Dictionary*).

The second time the word *telegraph* is mentioned is in footnote 6 to chapter 4, and was contributed by the translator: "Railroads and the telegraph being new in his day, S.K. constantly referred to them as wonders" (p. 104). McLuhan's point, in any case, had nothing to do with Kierkegaard's opinion of telegraphy, but only that he knew about it and (therefore, according to McLuhan's theory) was made to think in figure/ground relationships.

THE BELLY SPEECH IN *CORIOLANUS*

In a discussion of how artifacts, as media of communication, transform or change our sensibilities, McLuhan gives the example of a chair. Each part of a chair is named for a part of the body: feet, legs, seat, back, arms. Each part of the body in contact with the relevant part of the chair is "systematically numbed," we are told, as the chair "diverts energy" from it. Without pausing to think of the meaning of the word *numbed* in this context, we read on: "Are nails an extension of fingernails? of teeth?" (*Laws*, pp. 117–18). Is this to say, by its juxtaposition, that the parts of the chair are extensions of the relevant parts of the body? Immediately we learn that artists explore changes in "sensibility" (*Laws*, p. 118). An example from Shakespeare is used to illustrate this action. We expect to find information on some sensory change caused by an artifact. The example given is from *Coriolanus*, act 1, scene 1, lines 137–43.

In the following excerpt, I shall provide lines 134–64. They are spoken by Menenius Agrippa as an explanation to the mutinous citizens of how government works. Menenius compares the parts of the body of the state to the parts of the human body. All the body's members have rebelled against the belly because it did nothing but receive food and comfort. The belly responded thus to the criticism:

> "True is it, my incorporate friends," quoth he,
> "That I receive the general food at first,
> Which you do live upon; and fit it is,
> Because I am the store-house and the shop
> Of the whole body: but, if you do remember,
> I send it through the rivers of your blood,
> Even to the court, the heart, to the seat o' the brain;
> And, through the cranks and offices of man,
> The strongest nerves and small inferior veins
> From me receive that natural competency
> Whereby they live: and though that all at once,
> You, my good friends,"—this says the belly, mark me,—
>
> *First Cit.*: Ay, sir; well, well.
>
> *Men*:   "Though all at once cannot
> See what I do deliver out to each,
> Yet I can make my audit up, that all
> From me do back receive the flour of all,
> And leave me but the bran." What say you to 't?
>
> *First Cit.*: It was an answer: how apply you this?
>
> *Men*: The senators of Rome are this good belly,
> And you the mutinous members; for examine
> Their counsels and their cares, digest things rightly
> Touching the weal o' the common, you shall find
> No public benefit which you receive
> But it proceeds or comes from them to you
> And no way from yourselves. What do you think,
> You, the great toe of this assembly?
>
> (Shakespeare, n.d.)

Menenius makes sure his comparison is clear by working it out in the lines beginning "The senators of Rome are this good belly." The only way Shakespeare can be exploring the hidden effects of an artifact is if we consider the senators the artifact, and the benefits coming from them the hidden ground. But if this is his emphasis, why comment that the court is the heart of the state when the point is that the belly feeds all parts "Even to the court"? If we are supposed to see a similarity between Shakespeare's analogy and the action of the parts of a chair on the parts of the body, surely that comparison is inappropriate. There is an analogous relation of the parts of the chair to the parts of the body—*that's* a similarity—but neither has anything to say about transforming our sensibilities.

THE EAR, TOO, SUPPRESSES GROUND

Logical errors crop up far too often in this "new science" of McLuhan's. For instance, it is said that only the sense of vision can pick out the main object of attention from its background (*Laws*, p. 15). Surely the ear can suppress great quantities of (back) ground when pressed to intense activity. One need only listen to a tape recording made of the sounds in a room or restaurant, sounds that one had not heard at the time, to realize just how good the ear is at suppressing ground and isolating particular sounds (figures).

One of the qualities of the alphabet, we are told by McLuhan, is its ability to separate the senses from each other. The ear also separates figure from ground and separates the senses, inasmuch as one can hear sounds without seeing their source (Who has seen the wind?). If vision separates the senses—sound, smell, and touch are absent from a page of print—then surely sound alone, as on a tape recording (the comparable artifact to a page of print), separates the senses of smell, touch, and sight in the same way, when thus pressed to intensity of operation.

MANY MEDIA, MANY EFFECTS

For the sake of the argument in this section, let us grant some validity to the major hypothesis that media have effects on the psyche—irresistible effects that numb or enhance one or another of the senses. One wonders, then, just how often the effects of one medium are cancelled out by the effects of others. For instance, the "tetrad" for the "Law of New Genetics" says that one-to-one matching is enhanced, as well as the "mechanical code–view of life" (*Laws*, p. 176). We have previously been told that, in the phonetic alphabet, the letters had to be made free from ambiguity and that this was accomplished by one-to-one matching of sign and sound (p. 14). This led to a visual space bias in thinking that resulted in the geometrical model of Descartes, which was a mechanist outlook and built on the main characteristic of visual space: the "detachment of figures through ignoring or suppressing ground" (p. 27). With the coming of the telegraph and other electrical devices, the mechanical paradigm was replaced by a "field-mosaic approach" (p. 39). Notice, though, that the mechanical view of life enhanced by the new genetics would seem to cancel out the effects of the electric media.

However, the strongest argument for effects cancelling each other is the fact that, amid all the electronic speedup, reading is still taught in the schools, literacy is more important than ever, and computer printouts need to be read. Under the theory itself, clear-cut single psychic changes simply cannot happen.

McLuhan realized that the electric media were not having the effect he claimed they *must* have. Here is the strong side of his theory: "The effects of technology do not occur at the level of opinions or concepts, but alter sense ratios or patterns of perceptions steadily and without any resistance" (McLuhan, 1964, p. 18). How technology altered sense ratios was worked out in the media charts in his *Reports on Project in Understanding New Media* (McLuhan, 1960a). (An analysis of these charts can be found in Appendix II.) In *Laws of Media*, technology is broadened to include all human artifacts.

In all his works, McLuhan insisted that our electric world has returned to the acoustic space of preliterate cultures, yet there are three places in *Laws* where the purportedly irresistible nature of technology effects is contradicted.

1. "Acoustic space is a complete contrast to visual space in all of its properties, which explains the wide *refusal* to adopt the new form" (*Laws*, p. 33, emphasis added).

2. "Still, the overwhelming pattern of procedures in the Western world remains lineal, sequential, and connected in political and legal institutions, and also in education and commerce" (*Laws*, p. 80). [If the Western world's institutions are still—after more than a hundred years of electric communication—lineal, sequential, and connected, then the question is surely begged regarding the strength of the effects of the media.]

3. And we also learn, in the end, that these effects are not necessarily inevitable—that technological determinism imposes new cultural effects "willy-nilly" only when users of the media are "well-adjusted" or "sound asleep." The psychic effects of the media are not inevitable when there is a "willingness to pay attention" (*Laws*, pp. 127–28).

McLuhan's own solution to the imbalance of effects of the dominant medium supports the thesis of this section: if there are many media, the effects of one will play off against another. In *Understanding Media*, McLuhan wrote:

It is the theme of this book that not even the most lucid understanding of the peculiar force of a medium can head off the ordinary "closure" of the senses that causes us to conform to the pattern of experience presented. . . . To resist TV, therefore, one must acquire the antidote of related media, like print. (McLuhan, 1964, p. 329)

This contradicts the admonition to "pay attention," since "not even the most lucid understanding . . . can head off the . . . closure of the senses." I think this means that no amount of understanding will help unless something is actually done to remedy the situation.

I have suggested that there is sufficient contact with print (certainly in the Western world) to counteract the electric media. McLuhan, in the following, would seem to agree.

The TV thing itself is very, very polluting. It goes right into the nervous system. The problem is how literate is your society, your family circle, your immediate circle. Your child is coming out in an intensely literate world, so he can take a fair amount of TV without too much harm. But to the ordinary kid without a lot of literacy TV will just turn off any possibility of left hemisphere. (in Baldwin, 1977, p. 9)

Thus it is a question of just how much "literacy" will do the trick.

There is also the question of when television is no longer the television McLuhan analyzed in *Understanding Media*, where he said, "The TV image is *now* a mosaic of light and dark spots which a movie shot never is, even when the quality of the movie image is very poor" (McLuhan, 1964b, p. 313). In *Culture Is Our Business*, McLuhan predicted that "TV will produce a reversion to civilized book values by sheer reversal of itself" (1970a, p. 332).

When I say that the variety of media in our society cancel out the psychic effects postulated by McLuhan, I do not mean to suggest we do not need to study the social effects of media. When McLuhan said we have to pay attention and be aware of the effects of the media, we can agree wholeheartedly. But in saying this, he also says that the effects of the media do *not* alter our sense ratios or patterns of perception without resistance. I have shown that they do not alter our sense ratios at all.

THE MESSY ARTIST

It is possible to see the theme of this chapter as illustrative of a lack of intellectual rigor on McLuhan's part. Nor might he have objected. In one of his letters, McLuhan wrote, "The artist has to live in messy circumstances in order to keep his senses in play" (in Molinaro, Mc-Luhan, and Toye, 1987, p. 339). Part of the problem was his (messy?) style of thinking—the use of what he called "probes," which were ideas thrown out for discussion. His conversation was his workplace. Philip Marchand reported McLuhan as saying, "I do a lot of my serious work while I'm talking out loud to people. . . . I'm feeling around, not making pronouncements. Most people use speech as a result of thought, but I use it as the process" (1989, p. 58). Since much of his written work was dictated to his secretary, the aura of conversation was maintained in print.

Another reason for McLuhan's intellectual "messiness" was his dislike of "expanding on a subject in the sense of giving examples or otherwise underlining his point" (Marchand, 1989, p. 109). This attitude would militate against the search for evidence. Further, he was "never interested in finishing anything—certainly in the sense of polishing off something" (p. 70). The lack of polish shows not only in lack of clarity, but also in lack of consistency.

These lines from Kierkegaard's *Concept of Dread* are apropos:

By thus failing to let the scientific call to order be heard, by not being vigilant to forbid the individual problems to hurry by one another as though it were a question of arriving first at the masquerade, one may indeed attain sometimes an appearance of brilliancy, may give sometimes the impression of having already comprehended, when in fact one is far from it, may sometimes by the use of vague words strike up an agreement between things that differ. This gain, however, avenges itself subsequently, like all unlawful acquisitions, which neither in civic life nor in the field of science can really be owned. (Kierkegaard, 1944, p. 9)

4

The Language of Artifacts

At the beginning of *Laws of Media*, we learn that "one fundamental discovery upon which this essay rests is that each of man's artifacts is in fact a kind of word, a metaphor that translates experience from one form into another" (p. 3). Artifacts include anything made by humans, such as tools, engines, spacecraft, computers, theories, philosophical systems, remedies for diseases, styles of painting, and so on. McLuhan had made the suggestion very early in his media career. In *Report on Project in Understanding New Media* (McLuhan, 1960a), we find him saying, "We are obliged to learn the language of objects, and especially of those objects that are media" (p. 13); and foreshadowing that, in "Culture without Literacy" (McLuhan, 1953): "it is necessary to regard not only words and metaphors as mass media but buildings and cities as well" (p. 123).

In conjunction with this 'language of objects' concept, there is the theme, which runs through *Laws of Media*, about the need to use language precisely. Indeed, one of the goals of the tetradic system employed in describing the laws is to work out an exegesis of the language of artifacts. The laws of media provide the etymology and the exegesis of artifacts as words or metaphors. The introduction to *Laws* is prefaced by a quote from T. S. Eliot's "Little Gidding" to the effect that, since speech is the concern of the poet, then purifying the "dialect of the tribe" is the poet's responsibility. One gets the definite impression that this is what McLuhan had in mind. In a discussion of Francis Bacon and Giambattista Vico, he noted that many of the problems of civilization are caused by language. It is the job of the poet to cleanse these "Augean stables" (*Laws*, p. 85).

Teaching us the language of objects (purifying the dialect of the tribe) is the enterprise of *Laws of Media*. The 'laws' are applied to human artifacts to discover which parts of the body or which modes of thinking are "extended or stressed" and in which way (p. 117). Since McLuhan called objects 'words,' he felt that an etymological approach to these 'media' was appropriate. That is, the effect on human psychology and social organization could be discovered by tracing the history of these 'words' and by analyzing their component parts (and thus purifying them?). All human artifacts are extensions of humanity, just as speech utterances are extensions or "outerings"; and so all artifacts can be studied as a form of speech. The difficulty arises, as we shall see, because these 'words' are not just plain ordinary words, but metaphors—and metaphors are open to multiple interpretations. This language of artifacts is every bit as subject to individual interpretation as every other language, and McLuhan ultimately recognized this at the end of the book. He remarked that the analysis of any artifact or subject could result in a number of different tetrads, so that the question about which is right is "meaningless" (p. 238). This would seem to negate the usefulness of the laws in helping us come to an understanding of the language of artifacts; yet McLuhan's aim seems to have been to be precise, to purify the language of media as the poet purifies the language of the tribe.

Not everyone thinks that the goal, or even one of the goals, of poets is to purify the language; but McLuhan came by that view naturally—not only from T. S. Eliot and Ezra Pound, but from his experience at Cambridge (1934–36) where he was influenced by F. R. Leavis and I. A. Richards. Richards was already famous for the book he coauthored with C. K. Ogden, *The Meaning of Meaning* (1923), part of the subtitle being *The Science of Symbolism*. Richards's *Practical Criticism* (1929) reported an "experiment," one of the aims of which was "to prepare the way for educational methods more efficient than those we use now in developing discrimination and the power to understand what we hear and read" (p. 3). Richards liked to break things into parts, and at one point in *Practical Criticism* he identified four kinds of meanings: "It is plain that most human utterances and nearly all articulate speech can be profitably regarded from four points of view" (p. 175).

Leavis, too, focused on words: "A novel, like a poem, is made of words; there is nothing else one can point to" (1933, p. 16). Criticism must be, he wrote, "a matter of sensibility, of responding sensitively and with precise discrimination to the words on the page" (p. 17). Leavis was also concerned with the larger effects of literary works, but language was clearly the fundamental element. He quoted approvingly the following "axiom": "the problem of language, the use of the medium in all its aspects, is the basic problem of any work of literature" (p. 16).

This is not to imply that McLuhan was responding to any of these specific principles, but more to the attitude toward the analysis of words and the things they embody.

To address the issue of the language of media, my procedure will be to describe the laws and the tetrad structure first. Then I will set the project in the context of the poet's role of purifying the language. That is, if it can be shown that poets do in fact purify the language, and if it can be shown that McLuhan is a poet, then it might be possible to say that the laws of media—as a kind of poetry (ch. 5 of *Laws* is called "Media Poetics")—could help to improve our understanding of the implications and effects of human artifacts.

On the other hand, if it is concluded that poets do not purify the language and that McLuhan is not a poet, but if it can be shown that he was a "kind" of artist (see the conclusion to Chapter 8), then it might be possible to identify the real value of the McLuhan oeuvre in the context of 'art.' If I *do* show that McLuhan is a poet—whether or not poets purify the language—we can then approach his work as students of poetry.

THE LAWS OF MEDIA—TETRADS

The laws are set out as four questions:

1. What does the artifact enhance or intensify or make possible or accelerate?
2. What is pushed aside or obsolesced by the new "organ"?
3. What recurrence or retrieval of earlier actions and services is brought into play simultaneously by the new form?
4. When pushed to the limits of its potential, the new form will tend to reverse what had been its original characteristics. What is the reversal potential of the new form? (*Laws*, pp. 98–99)

In an earlier exposition of these laws, Barrington Nevitt was somewhat briefer:

We can sharpen perception of the environment created by any artefact, old or new, software or hardware, by carefully studying what it does in its constantly changing "figure/ground" relations:
  (1) What does it amplify or enhance?
  (2) What does it erode or obsolesce?
  (3) What does it revive or retrieve of a similar nature that was obsolesced earlier?

(4) What does it reverse or flip into at the extremes of its potential? (Nevitt, 1981, p. 67)

Nowhere did Nevitt suggest that there was a lawlike quality to these questions. Instead, he quoted from McLuhan's 1951 work *The Mechanical Bride* about the possibility of applying "the method of art analysis to the critical evaluation of society" (in Nevitt, 1981, p. 67).

Loosely stated as hypotheses, the laws declare that human artifacts have four and only four effects, as follows: (1) some aspect of the physical, social, or psychological environment is amplified or thrown into position as a visible 'figure'; (2) some aspect is reduced or eroded or becomes less important; (3) some aspect that was of little importance, but that had in the past been important, becomes more important; and (4) the effect of any human artifact, when pushed to or used in the extreme, brings back effects opposite to those it had initially amplified (reverses into or creates effects similar to those it had earlier eroded or obsolesced).

An example might be useful. In *Laws of Media*, the laws are illustrated in the "tetrad" form—a display that divides the page into quadrants, one for each law, the main effects centered around the intersection of the axes, with explanatory phrases and quotations spread diagonally toward the corners of the page. One of the tetrads is for cigarettes (see Figure 4.1, from *Laws*, p. 134). We find that, in accordance with the first law of media, cigarettes enhance or amplify or intensify or accelerate or make possible "calm and poise." Thus, per the second law, they push aside or obsolesce "awkwardness, loneliness." At the same time, the third law says, they retrieve "ritual, group security"—a 'ground' previously obsolesced (not then present in the life of the individual, although it once was?). And as predicted by the fourth law, when pushed to the limits of their potential (extreme use), cigarettes reverse their original characteristics of calm and poise to bring "nervousness, addiction"—characteristics similar to those that the cigarettes had initially obsolesced, that is, awkwardness and loneliness.

A second example—the tetrad "Pollsters" (see Figure 4.2; in *Laws*, spread across pp. 168 and 169)—is a little more complex. Here there are "glosses" or statements and quotations designed to explain the suggested effects of the artifact. Pollsters, as an artifact, enhance or amplify "user curiosity and insecurity." The gloss "Who am I?—Let's take a poll" is a joke emphasizing both these "enhancements." Of course, one might argue that the users of polls are often asking the question 'Who are *they*?'

What is obsolesced or eroded is "privacy." The gloss for this reads: "Does the president really have 17 per cent more charisma than Campbell's soup?" What is retrieved that was previously obsolesced is the

Figure 4.1

CIGARETTE

calm and poise	nervousness, addiction
ritual, group security	awkwardness, loneliness

Source: Laws, p. 134.

Figure 4.2

POLLSTERS

i.e., the ground (audience)
becomes figure (statistical profile)

the audience becomes actor

Who am I? – Let's take a poll.

user curiosity
and insecurity

the many into
the one
(the typical)

tribal/corporate
state of
communal
awareness

privacy

Does the president really have
17 per cent more charisma than Campbell's soup?

The providence that's in a watchful state
Knows almost every grain of Plutus' gold,
Finds bottom in th'uncomprehensive deeps,
Keeps pace with thought, and almost, like the gods,
Does thoughts unveil in their dumb cradles.
(Shakespeare, *Troilus and Cressyda*, III, ii, 196 – 200)

The popularity poll as navigators
handbook for politicians?

Source: Laws, pp. 168–69.

"tribal/corporate state of communal awareness." The explanation for this is given as "The popularity poll as navigator's handbook for politicians?"

When pushed to extremes, an artifact's effects reverse. For pollsters, this would be the reverse of "user curiosity and insecurity." The reversal effect is presented as "the many into the one (the typical)," which is explained by two sentences: "the audience becomes actor," and "i.e., the ground (audience) becomes figure (statistical profile)."

Nevitt said the parts of a tetrad are "in analogical relation, like a metaphor: Retrieval is to Obsolescence as Amplification is to Reversal, or (C/B = A/D); and Retrieval is to Amplification as Obsolescence is to Reversal, or (C/A = B/D)" (1981, p. 70). What is reversed, at the extreme, will be similar to what had been obsolesced when the artifact was first "made." We need to stretch our imaginations to see the many into the one (the typical) as the opposite of user curiosity and insecurity, and as similar to privacy. (Debating these propositions case by case can only be counterproductive. Clarification is limited here to mere presentation.)

A quotation from Shakespeare's *Troilus and Cressida* (act 3, sc. 2, ll. 196–200) is used as a further gloss for user curiosity and insecurity and, by its placement on the page, also for tribal/corporate state of communal awareness.

> The providence that's in a watchful state
> Knows almost every grain of Plutus' gold,
> Finds bottom in th'uncomprehensive deeps,
> Keeps pace with thought, and almost, like the gods,
> Does thoughts unveil in their dumb cradles.
> (Shakespeare, 1969 [17th century])

Poetry as a gloss complicates the precise clarification of the artifact's effects because of the necessity to interpret the meaning of the lines. Glosses in prose can also cause trouble. For example, in the tetrad for television, a quote from Tony Schwartz's book *The Responsive Chord* (1973), is used as an explanation of the enhanced effect of TV. Schwartz had written:

Watching television, the eye is for the first time functioning like the ear. Film began the process of fracturing visual images into bits of information for the eye to receive and the brain to reassemble, but television completed the transition. For this reason it is more accurate to say that television is an auditory-based medium. Watching TV, the brain utilizes the eye in the same way it has always used the ear. With television, the patterning of auditory and visual stimuli is identical. (Schwartz, 1973, p. 16, quoted in *Laws*, p. 158)

This quote from Schwartz was very important to McLuhan. He constantly recommended the book (see McLuhan, 1974), and Nevitt used the same quote in his book on communication (Nevitt, 1982). Schwartz's reasoning was that, because the dots on the television screen are lit in sequence by the cathode ray, our eyes actually see these dots and send the impulses to the brain where the whole picture is put together. This he compared to the way we hear: "The ear receives fleeting momentary vibrations, translates these bits of information into electronic nerve impulses, and sends them to the brain. The brain 'hears' by registering the current vibration; recalling previous vibrations, and expecting future ones" (Schwartz, 1973, p. 12). Nevitt himself provided a contradictory interpretation of how the senses work, however, with a quotation from Jean Piaget on Gestaltist structures.

The Gestalt psychologists maintained that what is given is always from the start a whole, a structure within which sensations figure only as elements. The perceptual whole is the datum that calls for explanation: this is where the field hypothesis comes in. On this hypothesis, the incoming nerve impulses *do not strike the brain one by one, sequentially, for by the mediation of the electric field of the nervous system they almost instantaneously give rise to "forms" of organization.* (Piaget, quoted in Nevitt, 1982, p. 55, emphasis added)

Peter Drucker, also emphasizing the need for perceptual (as well as analytical) thinking, remarked that "we had begun to shift toward perception well before the computer. Almost a century ago, in the 1890s, configuration (Gestalt) psychology first realized that we hear 'cat' and not 'C' 'A' 'T' " (1989, p. 263).

This might not be sufficient evidence to invalidate Schwartz's theory; however, it certainly *questions* that theory, as does our commonsense perception that our eyes see television pictures as whole pictures.

The laws, as 'observations,' are supposed to be in the form of testable statements under Popper's principle of falsifiability. However, each human artifact—for which, according to McLuhan, a tetrad may be constructed—is a "kind of word, a metaphor" (*Laws*, p. 3); and metaphors are not normal entities for Popperian scientific investigation. Perhaps this is why which tetrad results are arrived at is a meaningless concern, in terms of right or wrong (i.e., falsifiability).

We are told in at least two places in *Laws of Media* that the tetrads are also supposed to predict (pp. 8, 16). The only illustrated tetrad where a prediction was possible—where the 'artifact' was not so far in the past as to allow its effects to be known by hindsight—was the "Einsteinian Space–Time Relativity" tetrad. Following a sequence of laws—Newton's first law of motion, which reversed into the second law, which reversed into the third law, which reversed into relativity—Einsteinian space–time relativity reversed into "the next law of Physics (not discovered yet)" (p. 214). It seems to me that a truly predictive mechanism ought to have been able to predict what the next law of physics would be.

Barrington Nevitt's description (1981) of the tetrad exercise was more appropriate. He did not see the laws as scientific, nor as predictive: "We can sharpen perception of the environment created by an artefact, old or new, software or hardware, by carefully studying what it does in its constantly changing 'figure/ground' relations" (Nevitt, 1981, p. 68). Constructing tetrads could sharpen perception of the effects of artifacts on the environment, but it would not be scientific. Would it be a purification of the language?

DO POETS PURIFY THE LANGUAGE?

Where does the idea come from that one of the tasks of the poet is to cleanse the Augean stables of the bias imposed by language? The source of the idea seems to be in Stéphane Mallarmé's poem in memory of Edgar Allan Poe—"Le Tombeau d'Edgar Poe," written in 1876. The basic message of the memorial is that Poe was unappreciated by his countrymen until after his death. The second line of the second verse is the one Eliot paraphrased in "Little Gidding."

> *Eux, comme un vil sursaut d'hydre oyant jadis l'ange*
> *Donner un sens plus pur aux mots de la tribu*
>
> (Mallarmé, 1920, p. 74)

The second line translates as "To give a purer sense to the words of the tribe." Why Eliot used the word *dialect*, which adds the connotation of a regional variety of the language, may well have been so as to distinguish the tribe's language as a dialect of language in general.

In this connection, Joseph Galland and Roger Cros offered a prose paraphrase by Jules Lemaître of "Le Tombeau d'Edgar Poe" because *"il semble incompréhensible à première lecture"* (Galland and Cros, 1931, p. 304). I quote the relevant lines only: *"La foule qui d'abord avait sursaute comme un hydre en entendent donner un sens nouveau et plus pur aux mots du langage vulgaire."* Here the words of the tribe are understood as *"vulgaire,"* the vernacular. With the reason for Eliot's choice suggested above, it is possible to read Lemaître's wording in the same way, the vernacular being a local or national language distinct from, for example, Latin when it was the international language of Europe.

McLuhan was well aware of this concern for language on the part of poets. In his essay "Edgar Poe's Tradition," McLuhan wrote that Poe "had the craftsman's contempt for verbiage masquerading as expression" (in McNamara, 1969, p. 212). In his contribution to the collected volume *An Examination of Ezra Pound*, McLuhan quoted Pound on the necessity for the "literati" to maintain clarity and vigour of "any and every" thought and opinion, for when their work "goes rotten," i.e., when their very medium, the very essence of their work, the application of word to thing goes rotten, i.e., becomes "slushy" and inexact, or excessive and bloated, the whole machinery of social and individual thought and order goes to pot. (Pound, quoted in McLuhan, 1950, p. 166)

What did Pound mean by "clarity and vigour"? Perhaps his best description is in his *ABC of Reading*.

In Europe, if you ask a man to define anything, his definition always moves away from the simple things that he knows perfectly well, it recedes into an unknown region, that is a region of remoter and progressively remoter abstraction. Thus, if you ask him what red is, he says it is a "colour." If you ask him what a colour is, he tells you it is a vibration or a refraction of light, or a division of the spectrum. And if you ask him what a vibration is, he tells you it is a mode of energy, or something of that sort, until you arrive at a modality of being, or non-being, or at any rate you get in beyond your depth, and beyond his depth. (Pound, n.d. [1934], p. 19)

The Chinese ideogram for red, Pound said, puts together "abbreviated pictures of ROSE/IRON/RUST/CHERRY/FLAMINGO" (n.d. [1934], p. 22). The idea being that the Chinese define the color red by specific examples.
    An even better example is found in William Manchester's biography of Sir Winston Churchill.

Like any professional writer, he [Churchill] takes his text through several drafts before it meets his standards; but even in its roughest stages it is free of cant and bureaucratic jargon. . . . One sure way of rousing his temper is to call a lorry a "commercial vehicle" or alter "the poor" to "the lower-income group." He wages a long, and, in the end, successful campaign to ban the civil service's standard comment "the answer is in the affirmative" to a simple "Yes." . . . In both conversation and dictation he uses words with great precision and insists that others do the same. (Manchester, 1988, p. 33)

This was a campaign against the slushy and inexact, the excessive and the bloated. Churchill was evidently as concerned about language as Pound, for Manchester reported that between the wars Churchill could not recall "any time when the gap between the kind of words which statesmen used and what was actually happening in many countries was so great as it is now. They were saying smooth things and uttering pious platitudes" (Manchester, 1988, p. 88). It is not only the poets who have the responsibility to use language precisely. It is everyone's responsibility.
    Eliot also noted the tendency of language to become less intelligible the further away the speaker got from the things people experienced in

their daily lives: "A local speech on a local issue is likely to be more intelligible than one addressed to a whole nation, and we observe that the greatest muster of ambiguities and obscure generalities is usually to be found in speeches which are addressed to the whole world" (1948, pp. 87–88). This was, perhaps, inevitable as the world shrank and wars and business became more widely international.

In any case, not all poets are good at expressing things clearly, and some of the greatest of them call forth entire literatures of interpretation. In what is itself a somewhat ambiguous passage, Eliot said, "I wish that we might dispose more attention to the correctness of expression, to the clarity or obscurity, to the grammatical precision or inaccuracy, to the choice of words whether just or improper, exalted or vulgar, of our verse: in short to the good or bad breeding of our poets" (1933, p. 25).

Perhaps if Eliot had read the following somewhat different opinion by the American poet Karl Shapiro, he might have considered that too much attention had been disposed to the "bad breeding" of poets.

Now it may be true that language is sacrosanct, but we can respect this belief only in the way in which we respect the savage's belief in amulets. The mischief, however, comes with those poets who pin the destiny of the world on the state of the language. It was Mallarmé who raised the battlecry about purifying the dialect of the tribe. . . . And this was done in an elegiac poem about Poe, of all people. Whatever else Poe did, he certainly did not purify the dialect of the American, or any other tribe. (Shapiro, 1953, p. 19)

Shapiro is clearly referring to Eliot and Pound, since the reference to "dialect" is to "Little Gidding" and the comment about "the destiny of the world" is to such sayings by Pound as those quoted earlier.

If Shapiro was doubtful about Poe's role in purifying the dialect of the tribe, what would he have thought of James Joyce in this context? It was to Joyce's *Finnegan's Wake* that McLuhan would turn whenever he made a discovery about media or sensibility, to find that "Joyce had been there before him" (*Laws*, p. x). No example is given, but *Finnegan's Wake*'s conundrums have not helped purify the language.

On the other hand, perhaps McLuhan did not mean precision in the sense of precise meanings, but something else, as indicated in this comment on Poe: "Poe brought morbidity into focus, gave it manageable proportions, held it up, not for emulation, but for contemplation" (in McNamara, 1969, p. 220). So McLuhan brought media into focus; and through his system of charts (McLuhan, 1960a) and through the tetrads, he tried to give them manageable proportions—not so much purifying the language, but identifying media as a kind of language that could be studied.

Concepts are necessary for contemplation. As Nevitt said, "concepts are essential for scientific thinking" (1981, p. 68). And any thinking that is going to be productive or effective must be done with concepts that have meanings shared by others engaged in the discussion, or there will be nothing but confusion. McLuhan was good at using words with his own meanings in mind. That was why, for instance, he had to explain what he meant by obsolescence.

I have been saying that the book and printing are obsolete for years. Many interpret this to mean that printing and the book are about to disappear. Obsolescence, in fact, means the exact opposite. It means that a service has been so pervasive that it permeates every area of a culture like the vernacular itself. Obsolescence, in short, ensures total acceptance and ever wider use. (McLuhan, 1970b, p. 28)

Yet the 'law' that says a new medium displaces or obsolesces a condition or a thing certainly seems to mean what we usually understand by obsolete—no longer used or useful. Some of the examples given in *Laws* confirm that meaning: "the vacuum cleaner obsolesces the broom and the beater: the dryer pushes aside the clothes-line" (pp. 99–100).

In order to get at McLuhan's real message, we have to accept that his use of language is not a tool for conveying precise meanings. As Richard Kostelanetz (1968) complained, many of McLuhan's statements were metaphorical and defied precise analysis. Such statements, Kostelanetz said, "corrupt the language of explanation" (1968, p. 222). Nevitt, out of his long association with McLuhan, helps to clarify McLuhan's use of words.

"The medium *is* the message" is a symbolist statement which highlights the effects of the medium by suppressing the fact that the user is *both* content and co-maker of the experience. In symbolist representations, the normal ground is either changed or suppressed in order to sharpen awareness of the figure. "All my writing is satire," said McLuhan, "intended to wake people up." (Nevitt, 1982, p. 146)

So when McLuhan said 'the medium is the message,' we were not to take that literally. It was just a way of catching our attention. Nevitt made this same claim for his own work, and what he said might help with McLuhan.

Although my approach stresses multi-sensory probes for exploration (like Sherlock Holmes), rather than established theories for application (like Doctor Watson), the print medium forces my communication to be *given literally* even when my intent is not to be *taken literally*. My chief concern throughout this book has been to throw light on the current ignorance of our communication ecology, rather than to shine the light of present knowledge in the reader's eyes. (Nevitt, 1982, p. 170)

TRANSFORMATION

What is problematic in the relationship between language and the reader, or between any medium of communication and the receiver, is indicated in McLuhan's theory of communication. In a letter, he wrote, "I have the only communication theory of transformation—all the other theories are theories of transportation only" (in Molinaro, McLuhan, and Toye, 1987, p. 505). One way of understanding the word *transformation* is that the receiver does not receive only the author's meaning, nor, always, all of it, nor exactly it, nor the dictionary meaning, but a mix of these and her or his own biography at a specific point in space and time. In this approach, the transformation is a transformation of meaning. But is that the transformation McLuhan was thinking about? For instance, he said, "Electric media literally translated us into angels. On the phone 'we are there' and 'they are here,' and so with radio and TV" (in Molinaro, McLuhan, and Toye, 1987, p. 422). Of course, these are hyperboles. We are *not* "literally" translated into angels, nor are we transported by phone from here to there. This is a metaphorical way of speaking. It is a way of using language to create interest and generate interesting thoughts, but it is not exact and it is not clear.

It is curious that, in these few remarks on his theory of communication as transformation, McLuhan did not specifically mention the psychic effects that media are supposed to have on individuals and societies (unless these *are* the effects). The closest he came was in a 1971 letter in which he said, "Again, the *message* of the things (pencil, chair) is the sum of the changes that result from their social use" (in Molinaro, McLuhan, and Toye, 1987, p. 424). But the user of a medium is not completely defenseless—for while the user is always the content, nonetheless effects derive from the fact that "the user is often very evasive, or very stupid" (p. 505). That is, the receiver is not on the end of an automatic system that has some effect willy-nilly. The deeply subjective nature of the process of language—and languages of any kind, including the language of artifacts analyzed by the tetradic laws—means that the receiver of any communication has something to say about or contribute to the meaning, or the effect, of the message.

Of course, the author is equally defenseless against the reader. Helen Gardner expressed wonder at "the sudden irruption of a kingfisher into "Burnt Norton", for the garden is so remote from any water" (1978, p. 38). What was the significance of the kingfisher? She learned that Eliot had seen the bird on a visit to Kelham and had been excited at the sight. It entered "Burnt Norton" simply because of that experience, just as, "when asked for the significance of 'autumn,' Eliot replied simply 'it was autumn' " (pp. 38–39). A footnote illustrates the natural tendency of readers—and not just readers of poetry, but human beings in any situation—to "read" meaning into everything.

> We should perhaps be a little chary of giving too defined a symbolic meaning to the "chill fingers of yew" in *Burnt Norton* and the yew tree at the close of *The Dry Salvages*. There *are* yew trees in the garden as there *is* a yew tree in the churchyard where Eliot hoped to be buried at East Coker. A letter from Eliot to Hayward . . . replying to Hayward's appreciation of *Ash-Wednesday*, suggests that even the yews there have a more personal than a deliberately symbolic meaning: "Perhaps the yew does not mean so much as you suppose. It happened to occur in two or three dreams—one was a dread of 'the boarhound between the yew trees' and that's all I know about it." This dream gave Eliot the beautiful enigmatic line in *Animula*: "Pray for Floret, by the boarhound slain between the yew trees." Of course, the question of what symbolic meaning yew trees had for Eliot at this time to make him dream of them remains a legitimate question. (Gardner, 1978, p. 39)

In any case, the number of variables capable of effecting psychic changes, or changes in perception, is vast: the progression of social and personal history, religion, politics, the variety of contemporary media (clay and stone in Sumeria and Babylon; papyrus and parchment in the Roman Empire; the oral tradition and a written medium in ancient Greece [Innis, 1951, p. 64]; print, radio, and television in the twentieth century); and the explosion of population since the sixteenth century cannot help but be significant factors. Edmund Glenn and Christine Glenn, for example, discussed the demand for codification of culture created by the growth of populations in various parts of the world, and how that really amounted to the development of abstraction (1981, pp. 16–17).

There is therefore no way of proving, scientifically, that some transformation or another has occurred from a single cause. Nevertheless, the idea that the medium—and not just the content of a message—needs to be taken into consideration is a crucial insight. Although the germ of the idea that 'the medium is the message' was contained in the work of Harold Innis (see Molinaro, McLuhan, and Toye, 1987, pp. 219–20), it was Marshall McLuhan who broadened the proposition to emphasize that 'the medium is *the* message' and who popularized *that* message. For Innis it was an insight; for McLuhan it was a startling insight. This insight contains an element of truth easily grasped by anyone: most simply, just that the radio *is* different from the book, and one senses the difference in the experience of either. But it is still an insight and is not a falsifiable statement in Popper's science. Nor is the 'language' of human artifacts analyzed by tetradic laws any less prone to the vagaries of interpretation than any other human language. But these laws do provoke contemplation of media as value-laden phenomena. McLuhan was a teacher of a certain kind—the kind who acts as a devil's advocate. Anyone who can say, "I don't agree or disagree with anything I say myself" (McLuhan, quoted in Pollak, 1966, p. 57), is a teacher trying to make you think.

5

McLuhan's Theory of Communication (and Other Similar Communication Theories that are not Technologically Determined)

In this chapter, I will outline McLuhan's theory of communication and then present examples of other communication theories that are similar but are not related in any way to the electric communication media as determining cause. The existence of these theories will provide evidence to show how McLuhan's technological determinism was built on accidental historical correlations. The chapter will conclude with a demonstration of how it is possible to link other technologies than communication media to get the same social, environmental, and psychic effects McLuhan claimed for the Gutenberg printing technology.

MCLUHAN'S THEORY OF COMMUNICATION AS TRANSFORMATION

The second chapter of *Laws of Media* is entitled "Culture and Communication: The Two Hemispheres." In it the McLuhan concepts of space—acoustic and visual—are merged with the characteristics being proposed as functions of the right and left sides (respectively) of the brain. As the chapter draws to a close, we discover that the Shannon–Weaver model of communication is "the basis of all contemporary Western theories of media communication" (p. 86). The quotation used to make the point that the theory ignores completely receivers or users as ground (p. 87) is taken from the first page of Shannon's section of Claude Shannon and Warren Weaver's 1949 text and is curiously incomplete.

What follows is the quote in *Laws* and then, after the slash, the rest of the Shannon sentence.

The fundamental problem of communication is that of reproducing at one point either exactly or approximately a message selected at another point. Frequently the messages have meaning;/ that is they refer to or are correlated according to some system with certain physical or conceptual entities. These semantic aspects of communication are irrelevant to the engineering problem. (Shannon and Weaver, 1949, p. 31, cited in *Laws*, p. 87)

It is Weaver's "imaginative" model that includes semantic content and human receivers and that can be accused of "a kind of literal *matching* rather than resonant *making*" (*Laws*, p. 86). I have constructed a diagram from Weaver's description (see Figure 5.1).

This is the 'matching' communication model, so delimited when Weaver wrote that the problem of semantic coding must take semantic noise into account, the goal being "an adjustment of original message so that the sum of message meaning plus semantic noise is equal to the desired total message meaning at the destination" (Shannon and Weaver, 1949, p. 26).

In any case, the so-called Shannon model has long been recognized as inappropriate to human communication. Ross A. Eaman noted that Wilbur Schramm, in 1955, "more or less exhausted the possibilities" of extending Shannon's concepts to the study of mass communication, and "in so doing inadvertently made clear the limitations of Shannon's mathematical model for the study of mass media" (Eamon, 1987, p. 12). Stephen Littlejohn identified literature of the 1960s and 1970s that found Shannon's theory provided "practically no help in understanding everyday communication" (1989, p. 50). Not that the bullet or hypodermic-needle models of communication disappeared completely, for that concept of communication—the sender wanting the receiver to get the exact message being sent—is very appealing. It was not until the 1980s that communication models took into account interpretive behavior, particularly on the part of the receiver—although the fact of this interpretation was long known.

Ironically, the bullet or transportation model is peculiarly appropriate for McLuhan's idea that the technological structure of a medium has an effect automatically ("willy-nilly") on the human brain. It was this idea of the automatic irresistible impact that caused workers in the field of communications to categorize McLuhan as a technological determinist. Werner Severin and James Tankard discussed McLuhan's "media determinism" in which "the content of mass communication doesn't matter" (Severin and Tankard, 1988, p. 315). Melvin DeFleur and Sandra Ball-Rokeach (1989) were still reading McLuhan as having said that

Figure 5.1
The Shannon–Weaver Model of Communication

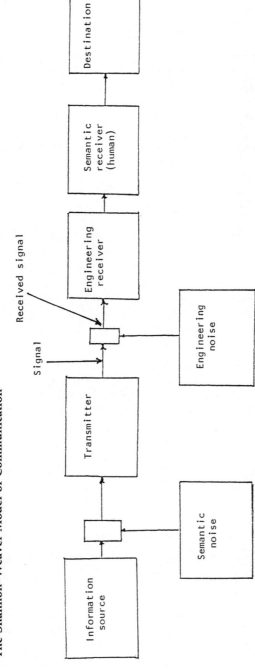

Source: Constructed by the author from Weaver's description in Shannon and Weaver, 1949.

"technology alone determines how people encounter and respond to the mass media" (DeFleur and Ball-Rokeach, 1989, p. 184), and "the content has no impact on audiences" (p. 185). Eaman classified him as an "assured technophile" who believed "that the electronic revolution in communication has modified human sensibilities and improved human relations" (1987, p. 151).

Stephen Littlejohn was more perceptive.

In the 1970s, McLuhan's teachings changed substantially. In his earlier works he strongly implies that the form of media in society *affects* or causes certain modes of perception on the part of society's members. In his later teaching he seems much less certain of this causal link. Instead, McLuhan says that media resonate with or reflect the perceptual categories of individuals. . . . Media forms do not cause but bring out modes of thought that are already present in the individual. (Littlejohn, 1989, p. 256)

Littlejohn saw that McLuhan's theory was unorthodox, that "his work is mostly artistic-historical-literary treatment and does not constitute a theory in the standard sense," yet his ideas "are valuable in that they point to the importance of media forms in society, but they do not give a realistic picture of the variables involved in the effects of media forms" (Littlejohn, 1989, p. 255). This last is basically what Toby Goldberg (1971) found in reviewing the positive comments on McLuhan just at the peak of his notoriety.

None of this recent literature on communication theory referred to McLuhan's letters, and yet it is in the letters that we get definite statements about a communication theory. In a letter written in 1973, for instance, he said, "What is called 'communication theory' today is merely the transportation of data from one machine to another machine" (in Molinaro, McLuhan, and Toye, 1987, pp. 467–68). This was a development from Herbert Krugman's 1970 brain-wave studies report (see Chapter 2), from which McLuhan quoted in a letter in 1971:

The *old* (communication) *theory* was concerned with the fact that the *message was transported*. The new *theory* must be concerned with the fact that *the viewer is transported, taken on a trip*, an *instant trip*—even to the moon and beyond. (Krugman, 1970, p. 18)

Krugman could only have been referring to the brain wave activity of his lone subject—that this *physical* response was equivalent to taking a trip to whatever scene the television picture showed ("the moon and beyond"). His conclusion was as much exaggeration as anything concluded by McLuhan.

McLuhan clearly kept thinking about his communication theory, and he qualified it in another 1971 letter: "The meaning of pencil, or the chair I use is the interplay between me and these things. . . . Thus, I have added two features to 'the medium is the message,' namely the content and the meaning" (in Molinaro, McLuhan, and Toye, 1987, p. 427). The 'message' is the sum of the changes that result from social use—the transformations in society that have come about through the use of an object ('medium').

The transformation, therefore, is in the world (i.e., media—human artifacts—have some impact on what we do) and in our minds inasmuch as we change our ideas when we receive 'messages' from our artifacts. The single quotes around 'message' indicates that we do not normally use that word when we mean to say, for example, that technology has an *influence* on what we do. A message is normally understood to be *intentional* and therefore coming from a human communicator. In this version of McLuhan's theory, therefore, the receiver transforms the meaning of the message through interpretation. As McLuhan once wrote to the Toronto *Globe and Mail*, "The meaning, or content, is somewhat different for each of us. . . . When people share the same experience, each creates a totally different meaning for that experience merely by relating it to his own unique being" (McLuhan, 1972a). In the same process, the receiver is "transformed" inasmuch as there are alterations in his or her cognitive structures, attitudes, or beliefs. Not every message will have a strong impact. People don't like to change. Not only that, but most messages are humdrum everyday sorts of communications that slip past us and leave little or no trace.

OTHER THEORIES OF COMMUNICATION AS TRANSFORMATION

Ben Lieberman might have been justified in saying, "McLuhan is right to thrust out at the pipsqueak communication theories of academicians and at the smug assumptions of most of the media leaders. We certainly have no communication theory today that is anywhere close to encompassing the realities and ramifications of communications" (1967, pp. 222–23). At that time, the hypodermic needle theory of communication seemed to be the standard, or, rather, the conventional wisdom. But there were clues that individuals did not take in unadulterated form the messages they received. In 1511 Erasmus wrote, "After all, it is what a reader brings to a passage rather than what he finds there which is the real source of mischief" (1961, p. 176). And McLuhan would certainly have known Wordsworth's "Lines Composed a Few Miles above Tintern Abbey," in which the poet wrote:

> Therefore am I still
> A lover of the meadows and the woods,

And mountains; and of all that we behold
From this green earth; of all the mighty world
Of eye and ear, both what they half create,
And what perceive

(Wordsworth, 1891 [1798])

William James, too, opened a window on the individual interpretation of events and objects.

The essence of a thing is that one of its properties which is so *important for my interests* that in comparison with it I may neglect the rest. Among those other things which have this important property I class it, after this property I name it, as a thing endowed with this property I conceive it; and whilst so classing, naming, and conceiving it, all other truths about it become to me as nought. (James, 1890, vol. 2, p. 335)

If that isn't a theory of communication as transformation, nothing is. And it describes exactly the way McLuhan himself ordered everything he observed into his visual/acoustic categories.

There were, as well, formal theories of communication that denied the matching principle McLuhan placed in opposition to the principle of 'making'—the influence of individual interpretation on the incoming message. David K. Berlo describes an 'interpreter' model (in Ball and Byrnes, 1960). Wilbur Schramm edited a text—and it went into several editions over a period of nearly twenty years—in which he made such statements as the following: "We can accurately think of communication as passing through us—changed, to be sure, by our interpretations, our habits, our abilities and our capabilities, but the input still being reflected in the output" (1954, p. 8). This is a little more realistic than McLuhan's hyperbole: "each creates a totally different meaning for that experience" (1972a). Exaggeration was a stylistic device that McLuhan used, going from "somewhat different" to "totally different" in the same breath. Schramm restated the idea when he noted that any communicator:

must give up any idea he may have of communicating impartial and unassailable "facts." . . . There are no impartial "facts." Data do not have a logic of their own that results in the same perceptions and cognitions for all people. Data are perceived and interpreted in terms of the individual perceiver's own needs, own emotions, own personality, own previously formed cognitive patterns. (Schramm, 1972, p. 111)

Schramm, therefore, was well aware that the communicator has to know the audience (1972, p. 13).

We see, then, that McLuhan was unaware of this literature when he stated in *Laws* that all Western communication models are like the Shannon–Weaver model: "linear, logical, and sequential" (p. 90). The kind of communication model he required for the electric age would have to take into account the interrelationship of figure and ground, instead of concentrating solely on abstract sequence. We can get a good idea of what is meant by 'figure' and 'ground,' in this context, from a letter written in 1973.

Communication theory for any *figure* requires the including of the *ground* for that figure and the study of the interplay between the *figure* and its *ground*. When Q. D. Leavis did a study of *Fiction and the Reading Public*, there was an uproar because she had ventured to suggest that highly literate people could lead moronic lives through most of their waking hours. It is the only study ever made, in English, of a reading public. That is, the study of *ground* for the *figure* of the novel. The ordinary study concentrates on *figure* minus *ground*. i.e. the content of the novel is studied and the kinds of readers and their relation to the novel are ignored. (in Molinaro, McLuhan, and Toye, 1987, p. 467)

The readers of novels are the ground in this example; so any audience is ground for any communication, which would be the figure. The required theory of communication therefore must include the 'receiver' or audience as well as that which is communicated, and their interrelationships.

Before leaving the above quotation, two further comments are appropriate. First, it is not accurate to say that Q. D. Leavis's *Fiction and the Reading Public* (1965 [c. 1932]) was the only study ever made of a reading public. Several were available long before McLuhan's 1973 letter. I refer to William Gray and Ruth Munroe (1929), Douglas Waples, Bernard Berelson, and F. W. Bradshaw (1940), and Nelson Henry (1956). Leavis, in any case, sent her questionnaire to authors, not to the reading public. Most of her book is a comparison of the content of 'literature' and popular novels, newspapers, and magazines; and she showed little understanding of the reading public (the ground) when she could say of "fantasying" that "the form of self-indulgence specified here accounts for the immense success of novels like *The Way of an Eagle, The Sheik, The Blue Lagoon*, a more detrimental diet than the detective story in so far as a habit of fantasying will lead to maladjustment in actual life" (Leavis, 1965 [c. 1932], pp. 53–54).

Second, I must offer a Popperian refutation of the thesis that print-biased people assume a neutral process of information transfer between the content (figure) and the reader (ground). This is falsified by the two examples given by McLuhan himself: Q. D. Leavis and H. A. Innis. I think we might also include Lynn White Jr.—about whom McLuhan wrote, "He is sensitive to the psychic and social implications of each technological extension of man" (1964b, p. 180)—to say nothing of the above-cited authors who studied the reading public. But perhaps we must stop taking such exaggerations literally, and rather see them as stylistic devices to catch our attention. After all, as McLuhan's friend Bruce Powers said, "Take for example: 'The medium is the message.' Marshall really did not expect people to take this literally" (1981, p. 1890). Of course, people who do not want to be taken literally should not write books.

There are at least three communication models that fulfill McLuhan's requirements, and I will set them forth briefly. The first is found in Eaman's book, *The Media Society* (1987): "communication as the social construction of text." This grew out of the field of semiotics and the study of meanings in 'texts.' Eaman clarified what was meant:

A text may be defined as any artefact that possesses meaning by virtue of the way in which it has arranged certain symbols or signs in accordance with certain rules or codes. In this sense of the term, a text could refer to not only a string of words (or letters) placed on a page using a certain form of grammar, but also a film, a radio or television program, a concert, an opera, a work of art, and so forth. Moreover, texts include the products of popular culture as well as high culture. Billboards, rock music, comic books, and advertisements are also texts. (Eaman, 1987, p. 25)

McLuhan went further and included all human artifacts as 'texts'—containing meaning—and McLuhan's laws of media were intended to be the 'grammar' of these texts. Audiences, continued Eaman, "read" or make sense of different texts on the basis of their own social background and culture. They interpret any given text within a certain historical context (Eaman, 1987, p. 25). Texts contain more than one potential message, and the messages "decoded" by those who receive the text "are seldom the same" (p. 25). The model studies the process of making rather than matching, and the ground of receivers as well as the figures of content and medium.

A second communication model that fits McLuhan's requirements is that of W. Barnett Pearce and Vernon E. Cronen, who gave the following encapsulation of their "new concepts of communication": "The new idea is that communication is a form of social action that can best be studied as a process of creating and managing social reality rather than as a technique for describing objective reality. The new idea is fundamentally discontinuous from traditional Western thought" (1980, p. 61). McLuhan would surely have looked carefully at any idea that was "discontinuous from traditional Western thought." The essence of Pearce and Cronen's concept was that communication is "a form of action persons perform toward or in the context of others. Those actions are constituted by the meanings individuals have of them, and acts thus create as well as reflect the reality persons perceive and in which they live" (p. 75). The idea of receivers creating "the context that contextualizes them" (pp. 305–6) is similar to McLuhan's description of the 'content' of the electric light: "Whether the light is being used for brain surgery or night baseball is a matter of indifference. It could be argued that these activities are in some way the 'content' of the electric light, since they could not exist without the electric light" (1964b, pp. 8–9). As Pearce and Cronen said, "Communication is a type of action that must be understood in terms of the actor rather than linguistic referents" (1980, p. 78), that is, rather than the *content* of the message (brain surgery, night baseball). Not that Pearce and Cronen ignore content, since they are concerned with actions and the process of creating reality. This is the "coordinated management of meaning" that Leah Lievrouw and T. Andrew Finn (1990) found consistent with their own perspective. Pearce and Cronen are not alone in holding such "non-Western" views.

Brenda Dervin (1981, 1983) of the Department of Communication, Ohio State University, originated a theory of 'sense-making' that complements the work of Pearce and Cronen, and that constitutes a third model fulfilling McLuhan's requirements. Dervin set out the Shannon–Weaver model in these terms:

The assumption—that messages should have a direct impact—rests on a number of other implicit assumptions. It assumes, for example, that messages can have a direct impact, that somehow they can get into receivers the same way they left the sources, and that they produce in all receivers the same impact. It assumes that a message is received the same way by source and receiver and by one receiver and the next receiver. It assumes that there is nothing unique about the receiver that will impact his or her use of the message. It assumes that there are no cognitive processes intervening between message and use. (Dervin, 1981, p. 74)

As an alternative, Dervin developed a constructivist theory of communication that assumes all information to be the sense made by individuals at specific moments in time–space.

Because the focus of Sense-Making is on constructings, research is directed to look not solely or primarily at things that traditionally have been defined as "communication." These traditional approaches have focused primarily on the transmitting of so-called objective, external, information from knowledgeable experts (e.g. scholars, educators, journalists) to those less knowledgeable (i.e. non-experts). Because of this, traditional approaches have focused not on constructing behavior but rather on source-using (and, in most recent work, networking). Sense-making, in contrast, focuses on how individuals use the observations of others as well as their own observations to construct their picture of reality and use these pictures to guide behavior. . . . Also related to the above is the idea that what is being predicted is not how people are moved by messages but rather how people move to make sense of messages. Thus, Sense-Making

searches for patterns in how people construct sense rather than for mechanistic
input–output relationships. (Dervin, 1983, pp. 5–6)

The process of 'making' could not be more clearly emphasized. Not only
that, but Brenda Dervin and Michael Nilan (1986) researched the literature of information science and reviewed those papers that have addressed the need to perceive the user and information communication
systems as a set of interrelated figure/ground processes based on the
concepts of communication presented above.

CORRELATING OTHER TECHNOLOGIES TO THE GUTENBERG EFFECTS

It is curious to speculate about McLuhan's response to these theories
of communication. In all likelihood he would have attributed their development to the effects of the electric media finally overcoming the
linear model epitomized by Shannon's mathematical theory of communication. But really all that it is possible to say is that there is a
correlation in historical time between the two, just as there was a correlation between the invention of the printing press and the rise of
individualism and a rational, empirical, nationalistic, and fragmented
culture. Pearce and Cronen made this interesting comment in their reference to McLuhan:

McLuhan's argument that print is a privatizing media that caused the development of individualism in Western thought is an intriguing—and untestable—
hypothesis. However, from whatever sources, radical, desacralizing humanism
characterized the transition from traditional to modern society, and individualism became the hallmark of fully modern society. (Pearce and Cronen, 1980,
p. 192)

There is, though, another explanation—other than McLuhan's—that is
more plausible and that does not include the Gutenberg galaxy.
    The invention of the printing press, McLuhan (1964b) told us,
"brought in" nationalism, industrialism, mass markets, individualism
(as different from the tribal community), detachment, disinterest (as "a
mark of the scientific and scholarly temper"), "fragmentation of knowledge and sensibility" (p. 175), and the desacralizing of "the world of
nature and the world of power alike" (p. 176). But if we read Lynn
White's *Medieval Technology and Social Change* (1962) carefully, we can
correlate other technologies than the printing press with the rise of
nationalism and individualism.
    White told how the stirrup was used to develop the armored horseman
and then the elite fighters we know as "knights." The "horseman with

lance at rest delivering a stroke with full momentum of his own body and that of his horse" (White, 1962, pp. 27–28) was possible only with feet firmly secured by the iron stirrup. This armed horseman, trained from childhood (and doing nothing else), was the backbone of the feudal class of the European Middle Ages.

This elite created a secular culture closely related to its style of fighting and vigorously paralleling the ecclesiastical culture of the church. Feudal institutions, the knightly class, and chivalric culture altered, waxed and waned; but for a thousand years they bore the marks of their birth from the new military technology of the eighth century. (White, 1962, pp. 28–29)

This thousand years also included the invention of the printing press and the burst of exploration after 1500.

The cost of outfitting a knight also created a class structure, fragmenting the community into a "warrior aristocracy and the mass of peasants" (White, 1962, p. 30).

The need to keep physically fit and to hone the skills of armed combat on horseback entailed long years of training and competition, leading to "rivalry among knights in feats of arms. . . . The new mode of combat, with its high mobility and fearful impact, opened fresh fields for individual prowess," so that "the emotional life of the chivalric warrior was highly individualized" (White, 1962, p. 32). As the violence of shock combat increased, heavier and heavier armor was built; the knight became unrecognizable under the equipment, and some means of identifying the individual underneath had to be developed. Thus, shields and pennons were personalized with armorial devices, increasing the emphasis on the individual.

Another invention made during the Middle Ages supported these changes—all of which owed much to the opening of new iron mines—and that was the heavy plough, which made the scratch-plough (essentially a large digging stick) obsolete. White described the new plough as follows:

Unlike the scratch-plough, the share of which simply burroughs through the turf, flinging it to either side, the heavy plough has three functioning parts. The first is a coulter, or heavy knife set in the plough-pole and cutting vertically into the sod. The second is a flat ploughshare set at right angles to the coulter and cutting the earth horizontally at the grass-roots. The third is a mouldboard designed to turn the slice of turf either to the right or left. (White, 1962, p. 43)

Because of its weight and the fact that wetter soil could now be worked, the heavy plough needed up to eight oxen to pull it. "Few peasants owned eight oxen," said White. "If they wished to use the new more profitable plough, they would therefore pool their teams"

(1962, p. 44). The end result was the growth of powerful village councils of peasants—the "seeds," along with feudalism generally, of nationalism. When you consider that "before the late 1700's there was probably no settled community in which at least nine-tenths of the population were not directly engaged in tillage" (p. 39), the impact of the long linear (very visual) furrows on the general imagination would be far more pervasive than the impact of print on those few who could read.

There is much more in White's descriptions of medieval nonprint technologies that correlates with McLuhan's claims about the psychic effects of print, such as this comment regarding the heavy plough: "once man had been part of nature; now he became her exploiter" (White, 1962, p. 56). But I only want to *indicate* the possibility of alternate "causes" (and none single) for these effects. There are others, also, who have described the changes brought about by technology. Chandra Mukerji (1983) agreed with the idea that the printing press was the first producer of mass consumer goods; but the fifteenth and sixteenth centuries also produced pins, pots, and ribbons. Mukerji attributed the growth of bias toward material things to the explorers bringing back new and strange objects, and then showed how this interest led to rational calculation and empiricism. Elizabeth Eisenstein admitted that McLuhan's work had stimulated her curiosity and led to the writing of her analysis of the complexity of change related to the printing press, but she also noted that he had "glossed over multiple interactions" (1979, p. 129).

In his (successful) effort to bring us to an awareness that the technology of communication carried effects ('messages') as a result of their *structure*, and not just their content, McLuhan erred on the side of simplicity, first, by overemphasizing the single technology of the dominant means of communication; second, by saying that this technology, and this alone, determined psychic effects; and third, by confusing correlation with cause and effect.

One might ask if McLuhan's correlations are not as valid as any others. I think they might be, if the variety of other facets of life are taken into account; for the correlation certainly exists. It was his literary style— using hyperbole, satire, and exaggeration, in a field usually the preserve of scientists and (tidy) scholars—that threw everyone off.

6

McLuhan's Method: The Dichotomies (and Other Dichotomies that are not Technologically Determined)

Other than the use of correlation, McLuhan applied a series of dichotomies to everything, the basic set being visual space and acoustic space. Later, the members of these two categories were incorporated into the left and right brain hemisphere terminology.

The use of dichotomies allowed McLuhan to make pronouncements on his observations quickly and easily, for he needed only to class events and phenomena into one of two categories. The ability of dichotomies to force contrasts—thus heightening, often by exaggeration, the point he was making—suited his goal of making people think, of waking them up to the hidden effects of technologies. Perhaps this method or, more accurately, this *style* was necessary, considering the number of people who had said similar things before him with little or no impact on society as a whole. I am thinking of James Carey's comparison (1981) of McLuhan with Lewis Mumford, and Richard Kostelanetz's list (1968) of precursors that included Lynn White Jr., Harold Innis, H. J. Chaytor's *From Script to Print* (1945), and Siegfried Giedion's *Mechanization Takes Command* (1948).

My intention in this chapter is to present the visual/acoustic space dichotomy in some detail, based on *Laws of Media* and the careful breakdown made by McLuhan's close colleague and friend Barrington Nevitt (1967). At times I will point to correlations with White (1962) and will refer to other descriptions of pre-electric cultures. Then I will identify other dichotomies that attempt to account for the effects McLuhan attributed to the technologies of communication.

VISUAL SPACE: PROPERTIES

McLuhan's basic tenet was that the development of the alphabet caused 'visual' space and the development of electric information transfer returned us to 'acoustic' space. What are the characteristics of visual and acoustic space? What attitudes and values do they "cause" in humans?

Visual space is a man-made artifact. It is continuous, connected, homogeneous, and static. Any simple mechanical device (e.g., the heavy plough, a suit of armor; see White, 1962, and discussion in Chapter 5 of this book) is a "model" of visual space in that it is made of static parts held together by connections, one part after another in linear fashion. The formal similarity to the alphabet is clear: meaningless parts joined into words and sentences by rules and connectors, and moving "linearly" from evidence to argument to conclusion, all the logical parts included to explain absolutely everything.

Perhaps the most important aspect of visual space is that it is the only form of space that is "purely mental" (*Laws*, p. 40). By this is meant that a euclidean line, for example, is just an idea, an abstract construct divorced from the real world. Euclidean geometry—with its triangles, rectangles, squares, and infinite lines—is a geometry of ideas, divorced from the round earth of obstructive trees and erupting mountains. McLuhan used a quotation from Fritjof Capra's book, *The Tao of Physics*, as illustration: "The structures and phenomena we observe in nature are nothing but creations of our measuring and categorizing mind" (1975, p. 292, quoted in *Laws*, p. 59). Thus, visual space is the mental world of the abstractions we use to analyze and organize experience.

It is called "visual space" because of the heightened use of the visual sense in reading and writing the phonetic alphabet. The visual is heightened because, with a phonetic alphabet, there is nothing pictorial; the imagination has to "fill in" the visuals. The act creates a *psychic* visual space. It is a 'space' that is in the mind. It creates an inner world abstracted from the outer world. It creates the *observer* of the outer world: the scientist and the exploiter of nature.

VISUAL SPACE: EFFECTS ON ATTITUDES AND VALUES

A person with a visual space (left brain) orientation tends to be an observer—detached, objective, individualistic, quantitative, using an historical approach that organizes the outer world for analysis, and engaging the scientific method to abstract figures from the ground of the outer world (nature) in order to make measurements. The following are the main characteristics of visual space. When you are reading this list of properties, I would like you to keep in mind the armored knight in his stirrups and the peasant behind his iron plough admiring his acres of furrowed earth—although anyone living in the Age of Exploration could hardly have been characterized by the last item.

- Linear, uniform, continuous unidirectional, rigidly connected—with definite boundaries, clear perspectives, specific goals, and private points of view
- Three-dimensional, with both "inside" and "outside"
- Containing and excluding
- Centers with margins
- Sequential, plodding, one at a time, consistent
- Analytic, fragmenting, specializing, centralizing
- Matching, reducing
- Filtering, classifying
- Separate particles, entities, or things—with individual properties and motivating forces
- Quantitatively measuring, extrapolating, and interpolating
- 'Breakdowns lead to breakups.'
- 'There is nothing new under the sun.' (Nevitt, 1967, p. 15)

ACOUSTIC SPACE: PROPERTIES

Acoustic space consists of resonant intervals, dynamic relationships, and kinetic or tactile pressure. Its structure is analogous to a sphere in which things and all the senses modify and coerce each other. It is multisensory. There is no possibility of an abstract concept such as infinity.

Perhaps the most significant aspect of McLuhan's acoustic space is its "natural environmental form" (*Laws*, p. 22). It is the space we usually think of when we use the word *space* (not, however, *outer* space). Even normal visual space is included, because we think of the space we see— and also sense in other ways—when we look around. It is the space we experience with *all* our senses.

Acoustic space is acoustic because it is the space of *oral* cultures. Interpersonal communication is mainly by ear, by listening. Electric information transfer is analogous to oral culture because the information moves as fast as words from mouth to ear in oral conversation: it is "instantaneous." It is this similarity of form (simultaneity) that encourages the equation of electric and oral cultures—both residing in 'acoustic space.'

ACOUSTIC SPACE: EFFECTS ON ATTITUDES
AND VALUES

The dominant personal characteristic associated with acoustic space is involvement—the multisensory impact, the experience of living face-to-face in an "oral" culture. Thus qualitative factors are more important, as are human relations and ecology (the caring rather than the conquering relationship with nature). Present concerns prevail, and historical antecedents are ignored. The following are the features of acoustic space:

• Nonlinear, nonuniform, discontinuous, from all directions, totally related—with neither boundaries, nor perspectives, nor goals, nor points of view
• Multidimensional, with neither "inside" nor "outside"
• Involving and including
• Centers without margins
• All at once, sudden, all-together, inconsistent
• Synthetic, integrating, generalizing, decentralizing
• Making, creating
• Exploring, revealing
• Interfacing, interpenetrating, interdependent fields, processes, and patterns—in constant interplay
• Qualitatively comparing, transforming, and combining
• 'Breakdowns lead to breakthroughs.'
• 'There's nothing more constant than change.' (Nevitt, 1967, p. 15)

The last characteristic seems not at all appropriate for primitive or preliterate cultures, where the prospect of change is ignored rather than abhorred. The opening paragraph of a novel by Barbara Kiminye about modern tribal Africa illustrates this particularly well:

A village which has remained virtually unchanged throughout the reigns of thirty-four consecutive Kabakas can hardly be expected to show any fundamental difference in the short space of two years, and so, on this, our second visit to Kalasanda, we are not terribly surprised to find that the only thoroughfare, that narrow, murram track sidling discreetly off the main Hoima road, and sneaking through Kalasanda to the adjoining village of Gumbi, is, if anything, even rougher and more anti-motorist than it was before. Anyone would think that Kalasandans had never heard of "Bulungi Wansi," for in vain does Ggombolola Chief Musisi appeal to their civic pride when it is a question of keeping the village's only link with a trunk road reasonably passable. "You'll never get anywhere at this rate," he constantly reminds them, and their usual reply, issued with infuriating complacency, is: "Well, where is it that we are supposed to be going." (Kiminye, 1966, p. 9)

McLuhan's problem—and his advantage—was that he was not in his own discipline. His field was English literature. The communications field and the field of the senses belong more to psychology and sociology. Since McLuhan's examples and his style were literary and yet were applied to psychological events (the psychic effects of the media), confusion could not help but result. His lack of background in the area under study caused a misuse of terms or the development of novel meanings for terms used differently by others. So 'figure/ground' and 'visual/acoustic space' as he used them were confusing to those who used them otherwise. As Kostelanetz pointed out, "McLuhan's use of abstract words such as 'myth' and 'archetype' is highly idiosyncratic—perhaps more metaphoric than accurate" (1968, p. 222).

The advantage he had, in terms of impact, was that he was not motivated to look at the psychological and cognitive aspects of communication through the theories and methods of those disciplines. He thus avoided the heavy scholarly language of "linear" argument and evidence. Academics in the relevant subjects simply could not understand the literary or artistic method, nor could they trust the results coming from such a patently unscientific style.

That style was attractive to the media practitioner because it was entertaining; "any phrase-making yokel can become a world center," McLuhan had said (Howard, 1966, p. 95). Further, *what* McLuhan was saying was attractive to media practitioners because it was about them and their business, and it was—or seemed to be—positive and approving. Navel gazing is an almost irresistible activity. But since the media people didn't really understand McLuhan either, he was basically an entertainment, a diversion. Thus, when he continued to *repeat* his message—when he was no longer new and news—his popularity faded. The media folk were, after all, 'acoustically' oriented—discontinuous and inconsistent. Philip Marchand noted that this was clear by 1970: "No longer did magazines feel compelled to do a piece on him. He had already been 'done' and there seemed nothing more to say" (1989, p. 220).

OTHER DICHOTOMIES THAT EXPLAIN EVERYTHING
BUT ARE NOT TECHNOLOGICALLY DETERMINED

As Joseph Bogen said when he assumed two types of intelligence, breaking the world into two parts "appeals for reasons of simplicity" (1977, p. 137). I have already analyzed the characteristics of the 'left and right brains,' which McLuhan adopted because they matched the qualities of visual and acoustic space. He did not examine the split-brain research carefully, nor would he have been interested in other dichotomous explanations of human action unless they could be made to match his own categories. But there *are* others, and they are grounded in something other than communication technologies.

Herman A. Witkin proposed two cognitive styles—field dependent and field independent—that are "bipolar" (1978, p. 28) or dichotomous, and that develop from the process of adapting "to the demands of the life situations with which they must cope" (p. 30). That is, they are not psychic effects caused by the media of communication, but by the "ecological forces to which they are subjected, and to which they must adjust" (p. 31). Witkin was careful to maintain a continuum between the extremes of the two styles, the clusters of skills having "their high and low levels at opposite poles of the field dependence—independence cognitive-style dimension" (p. 20). Thus, in comparing studies of "subsistence-level migratory hunting and gathering groups, on the one hand, with sedentary agricultural groups, on the other hand," he concluded that "members of migratory groups are likely to be *relatively* field independent and members of sedentary groups *relatively* field dependent" (p. 31, my emphasis).

The characteristics of field-dependent people are similar to those of preliterate oral or 'acoustic' types in McLuhan's system. The field-independent people are similar to McLuhan's 'visual' types.

Field-dependent people take their cues from the external community and so are more likely to prefer an interpersonal orientation, seeking emotional and physical closeness to others. They have been found to be more effective in reaching a consensus and more sensitive to social information. Since they are more likely to respond "to the dominant properties of the field as given" (Witkin, 1978, p. 22), they are also more likely to use a "spectator" approach in learning new concepts, similar to the synthetic and gestalt approach of McLuhan's acoustic individual—or, as in one item from Nevitt's list of acoustic space effects, "perceiving directly what is happening" (1967, p. 18).

The field-independent type prefers to keep people at arm's length, showing the individualistic characteristics of the visual person, more concerned with ideas and principles than people. This conforms to McLuhan's visual space individual: intellectual, with a private point of view. The field-independent person approaches the task of organizing a "field which lacks inherent structure" by "imposing a different organization on the field than the one it contains, or breaking up an organized field so that its parts are rendered discrete from ground" (Witkin, 1978, p. 22). This equates to the fragmenting, analytical style of McLuhan's visual type, isolating and separating figure from ground. As a learner, the field-independent person uses a hypothesis-testing approach, analyzing succeeding concepts in the light of hypotheses made about concepts already experienced—or, as in Nevitt's list of visual space effects, "judging indirectly through ideology or theory" (1967, p. 18).

Hunters—the epitome of the field-independent type—live in small bands, expecting every member to be able to do everything; so "role diversity is thus limited" (Witkin, 1978, p. 32). The solitary hunter has to be able to fend for himself. Agricultural people, as sedentary groups, develop elaborate social structures and "considerable role diversity," plus "conformity to social, religious, and political authority" (p. 33).

These characteristics are found in Nevitt's lists—the sensory preferences of acoustic space being corporate togetherness, as opposed to visual space's individual privacy and cool detachment. The social function preferences of the two types are for acoustic space—"playing a 'role' by involvement in an undertaking," and for visual space—"doing a 'job' as a bit of work" (Nevitt, 1967, p. 17). Witkin added that individual autonomy is "more typical of migratory groups" and that the greater social complexity in larger agricultural groups "makes for more social roles" (1978, p. 41).

In McLuhan's system of dichotomies, nonalphabetic cultures—such as the Inuit (Eskimo) and the Chinese—are acoustic, whereas alphabet cultures are visual. It is revealing that Witkin found no such split.

It is particularly impressive that the same pattern, encompassing ecology, social structure, socialization, and cognitive style, has appeared repeatedly among mobile hunting groups from widely separated parts of the world which probably never had contact with each other—for example, the Arunta of Australia, the Boat People of Hong Kong, the Cree, Athabascan, Ojibway and Carrier Amerindians, the Lapps, and the Canadian, Greenlandic, and Alaskan Eskimos. The contrasting pattern has been found among equally scattered sedentary agricultural groups—for example, southern Nigerians, the Temne and Mende of Sierra Leone, the Nsenga of Zambia, South African Bantu, Tsimshian Amerindians, the Haka of Hong Kong, and Fijian Islanders. These findings seem to support the theses that how people make their living is important in determining not only the social forms they adopt, but also the child-rearing practices they develop and the patterns of individual behavior they encourage. Perhaps this thesis finds particularly impressive support in the subsistence-level settings we have been considering because economic factors hold such great sway in these settings. (Witkin, 1978, p. 35)

Cognitive style (visual or acoustic; field independent or field dependent) is developed in accord with the requirements of life situations, not as a result of the media of communication. Witkin's thesis is supported by enormous quantities of research.

Another general dichotomy that corrals similar processes and predilections as McLuhan's and Witkin's is that of Edmund Glenn and Christine Glenn (1981). Briefly, they take 'associative' and 'abstractive' styles of reasoning, making sure we understand them to be relative rather than absolute terms, and apply them to various cultures. Associative reasoning is marked by arbitrary ties between informational units; whereas abstractive reasoning is marked by "(1) the definition of information which is relevant to a given situation" (i.e., distinguishing the figure from the ground) and "(2) the definition of the relationship between informational units" (p. 57)—"filtering, classifying" from Nevitt's list (1967). The associative mode is 'acoustic'; the abstract mode 'visual.'

To reinforce the relationship, Glenn and Glenn show that "preliterate and archaic cultures tend to be more associative and less abstractive than 'modern' cultures" (1981, p. 59). They also advance research to indicate that working-class people are more associative, identifying themselves through association with a particular group. Middle-class people "seek identity primarily through achievement" (p. 94). This dichotomy also holds for 'folkman' and 'urban man.' Like the hunter in Witkin, urban man can—at least minimally—survive in society "without ever depending on a friend or on close and affective relationships." Folk individuals "need human surroundings dominated by person-to-person relations" (p. 102). Folk man determines identity by association "based on immediately given experience, holistic, carrying for intimates the full histories of previous encounters." Urban man determines identity abstractly, "based on the conceptualization of roles" (p. 103). The acoustic individual is holistic and emotional. The visual individual prefers the analytic and the fragmenting of roles into (just a) job—the "hierarchy of authorities" of Nevitt (1967, p. 18).

Glenn and Glenn (1981), in a chapter on preliterate cultures, wondered if there were any cultures entirely "associative and pre-logical" and others that were entirely "abstractive and logical." Such cultures would be McLuhan's categories of literate and oral—visual and acoustic, respectively. Glenn and Glenn found examples of associative prelogical thought in the most advanced cultures, and concluded that most of the examples suggested "the two patterns coexisted in the same cultures" (1981, p. 211). That is, some logical thinking is needed to survive, and there is a general human need for affective and artistic creativity.

The cause of these modes of thought was seen to be the growth of population, bringing with it the amalgamation of small communities and the "resulting increase in contacts between individuals" (Glenn and Glenn, 1981, p. 48). In a sense, this is close to Witkin's life-situations thesis. We need to remember that in Europe the beginnings of population growth came, in part, out of the improvement in diet made possible by the heavy plough's ability to work wetter soils (White, 1962).

Glenn and Glenn linked their rationale to Emile Durkheim's thesis "that the development of abstractive thought is made necessary by increases in what he calls social density, that is to say the product of the size of a society by the mobility which prevails within it" (1981, p. 94). This does not mean that preliterates are incapable of abstraction, or that members of advanced cultures find it easy and natural. All cultures have their "men of action" and their "men of thought," always trying to clarify and expand knowledge.

In the case of small populations, as that of most preliterate tribal cultures, the men of thought may be too few to reach a critical mass which would permit the setting up of a social body the function of which would be to codify and to expand knowledge. In the great literate civilizations, which usually have much larger and more mobile populations, the critical mass may be reached. This may lead to the establishment of specialized institutions such as universities and think tanks in which thinkers of the civilization react among themselves, systematizing and expanding knowledge. (Glenn and Glenn, 1981, p. 219)

This description applies equally to Europe and to China.

PROBES AS MANIFESTS: MANIFESTS AS ART

One of the most famous, if not notorious, of McLuhan's dichotomies is the classification of media as hot or cool. 'Hot media' are those with 'high definition,' and 'cool media' are those with 'low definition'—the high definition of a printed letter versus the low definition of a written letter. Toby Goldberg took fifteen pages to discuss the various uses of these words, concluding that they were "the least satisfactory of all McLuhan's arguments and concepts" (1971, p. 384). In Nevitt's lists of the "analogical uses" of visual space we find "Hot media, such as print and film," opposite "Cool media, such as telephone and Black and White TV," in the acoustic space list (1967, p. 15). Goldberg found these categorizations "very confusing," and could not understand why McLuhan called paperback books cool and hardcover books hot. Earlier, Goldberg had listed the characteristics of cool media: "casual, retribalizing, communal, improvisational, avant-garde, primitive, socially participatory, active and producer-oriented" (1971, p. 371). Clearly, the paperback (the pocket book), which can be shoved easily into purse or pocket, is more "casual" than a hardcover book. As a matter of balance, Goldberg gleaned from McLuhan's writings these hot media characteristics: "specialist, explosive, fragmentary, individuating, detribalizing, fantasy-inducing, passive and consumer-oriented" (Goldberg, 1971, p. 371). After analyzing a large quantity of literature by and about McLuhan, however, Goldberg was not able to clarify further the meaning of these terms.

I think it is better to leave the details to McLuhan; he used words as he pleased, in his own way and with his own meanings, and he did so with assurance and flair. To understand McLuhan it is necessary to stand away from the "fine points" and grasp the broad generalizations. Otherwise, one drowns in illogic, contradiction, and a casual use of

facts. Henry Holorenshaw (1973) made a comment about Joseph Needham that is relevant.

One of the struggles which he most clearly remembers was in Christian litur-
giology itself, where he was captivated early by its wonderful symbolism yet
repelled by much of the phraseology, till he came to realize that the words were
a form of poetry, not to be dissected by the scientific scalpel or criticized by the
methods of the linguistic philosopher. (Holorenshaw, 1973, p. 5)

And so too must McLuhan's words be approached as a form of poetry.
   It need hardly be said that we do not live in a dichotomous world.
There is no either/or in the experience of the communication media. We
have always been oral and always will be. All other media are merely
add-ons. Nor is there an either/or in our experience of the world: we
hear, feel, smell, taste, and touch all day long. Humans are multisen-
suous beings who live not only in their minds and imaginations, but
also in the garden and the parking lot. Dichotomies are useful to high-
light models of experience, but those models are not experience. Nor
would McLuhan say they were. His goal was to awaken us to the effects
of media, and he went about it in the only way he knew (or could, or
liked).
   When Glenn and Glenn (1981) discussed language in terms of their
associative and abstractive polarities, they regarded associative languages as being mainly concerned with subject and object, that is, a
preoccupation with the accuracy of language in describing the observed.
On the other hand,

what abstractive languages do is to present statements of opinion as if they were
statements of fact. As such, they can be faulted, and it is precisely this fault
finding which sets in motion the intellectual curiosity which ultimately leads to
research. . . . Thus it calls for a critical examination of what is said. (Glenn and
Glenn, 1981, p. 86).

This is a neat description of McLuhan's style. He certainly "affirmed
more than is known" (Glenn and Glenn, 1981, p. 86), and he begs critical
examination. It was this sort of criticism he wanted when he said of an
early presentation of the laws of media that his purpose was "to invite
criticism, directed not at me or at my rhetoric, but rather at the substance
and contents of my thoughts" (McLuhan, 1975, p. 74). He sought criticism from the wrong sector. He was an artist, not a scientist, and every
once in a while he knew it. In a dialogue with G. E. Stearn (1967),
McLuhan said, "When I sit down to write about complicated problems
moving on several planes, I deliberately move into multi-sensual prose.
This is an art form . . . a serious art form" (Stearn, 1967, p. 285). What
could he possibly have meant by that?

When I wrote my article on McLuhan's media charts (Neill, 1973a; reprinted here as Appendix II), I sent a draft to McLuhan for comment. He gave it to Barry Nevitt, who made some notes for McLuhan and sent me a copy. This is what Nevitt wrote, in part:

Marshall, I have discussed the attached paper with Sam and pointed out that:
  (1) McLuhan charts were intended as *probes* to expose input/output *sensory* transformation via media.
  (2) They were enlarged to indicate not only "psychic" effects but also *physical* and *social*.
  (3) They are embryo *manifests* where the meaning lies in the gaps, not the logical connections. (Nevitt, 1973)

That is, as I read it, if there are no logical connections, one cannot say "This is connected to (implies, means) that." One can, however, ask the question "Are there any connections?" Such a question is asking about the gap where there might or might not be a link. So a 'manifest' is something that is intended to show, say, an effect, but as a manifest it is like a work of art: it merely shows. Its purpose is to "make manifest." Discussion is allowed, but the artist has done all that can be expected. To question the artist is to get a reply such as "It means whatever you think it means." Or, as we have already learned about the tetrads, "the question as to which is the right one is meaningless" (*Laws*, p. 238). Indeed, the tetrads can be seen as mature, as opposed to embryo, manifests or probes.

A probe is a question. In McLuhan's case, it is made as a statement: 'It's in here. No, over here. Maybe in this area.' It's like needles probing the body of society, except that McLuhan's needles are phrases and pairs of words (hot or cool, visual or acoustic)—manifests, pieces of art. As art in words, therefore, McLuhan's aphorisms and dichotomies are poems. They are creations to be considered, even appreciated. The tetrads are do-it-yourself poems—"media poetics," as the last chapter of *Laws* is called. They perform the same role as the pack of cards called "Distant Early Warning," published as part of McLuhan's *DEW-LINE* newsletter in 1969. On each card was a joke or aphorism intended to spur thought in brainstorming sessions. Marchand explained, "The player was supposed to think of a personal or business problem, shuffle the deck, select a card, and apply its message to the problem" (1989, p. 216). These are some of the "messages": "Is there a life before death?" on the five of hearts; "To the blind all things are sudden," on the jack of diamonds; "With data banks we are taped, typed and scrubbed," on the nine of clubs. The tetrads, with the laws as rules, are a more serious game, each 'conclusion' being a 'manifest' to think about.

Because he was making manifest what he "saw," McLuhan consistently protested that his work was rooted in percepts, not concepts (*Laws*, p. 11). In that sense, probes and manifests are examples of what Archibald MacLeish in his "Ars Poetica" (1926) said a poem is; namely, a poem should "be." That is, it should exist as an art object, rather than a construction of meanings. However, we cannot ignore the fact that words do have meanings, and we have C. S. Lewis's comment on the MacLeish conundrum: "But modern poetry, if it 'says' anything at all, if it aspires to 'mean' as well as to 'be,' says what prose could not say in any fashion" (1961, p. 97). Lewis went on to clarify the difference between 'meaning' and 'being,' and it is something to keep in mind when I come to analyze the tetrads as poetry.

A work of literary art can be considered in two lights. It both *means* and *is*. It is both *Logos* (something said) and *Poiema* (something made). As Logos it tells a story, or expresses an emotion, or exhorts or pleads or describes or rebukes or excites laughter. As Poiema, by its aural beauties and also by the balance and contrast and the unified multiplicity of its successive parts, it is an *objet d'art*, a thing shaped so as to give great satisfaction. From this point of view, and perhaps from this only, the old parallel between painting and poetry is helpful. (Lewis, 1961, p. 132)

Any hypothesis is a kind of probe, a conjecture. But in normal scientific work it is not considered a work of art—although Paul Dirac, the discoverer of antimatter, all but said that it is. In answer to Horace Freeland Judson's question "How does one recognize beauty in a theory?" Dirac replied, "Well—you feel it. . . . Just like beauty in a picture or beauty in music. You can't describe it, it's something—and if you don't feel it, you just have to accept that you're not susceptible to it. No one can explain it to you" (quoted in Judson, 1980, p. 199). Perhaps this feeling—that others were not susceptible to his 'percepts'—prompted McLuhan to say, in response to William Henry Venable's critique (1976) of the laws of media, that there was "no point of contact" (McLuhan, 1976, p. 263). As one reporter remarked about McLuhan, "He makes a habit of saying that somebody like Plato, Kant, Einstein, Toynbee, Spengler, Mumford, 'failed to grasp' what he grasps so easily" (Cort, 1966).

Throughout *Laws of Media* we find the claim that artists are the antennae of the race. McLuhan clearly saw himself as an antenna (the 'distant early warning') and as an artist (his multilevel prose as a serious art form). What does it mean to be an antenna of the race? I will explore that attribution in the next chapter.

7

The Artist as Antenna

ORIGIN OF THE PHRASE

At several places in *Laws of Media* (pp. 6, 47, 76) we learn that artists are the 'antennae of the race' and have already tuned into the new electric ground and begun exploring discontinuity and simultaneity. The words *antennae of the race* are always set in single quotes. Where did McLuhan get that phrase? What does it mean?

Having studied the work of Ezra Pound and written an article in 1950 called "Pound's Critical Prose" (McLuhan, 1950), McLuhan very likely had read this phrase in Pound's essay "The Teacher's Mission" (Pound, 1954c), written in 1934 in the *English Journal*, where it is in the lead sentence. He might also have seen it in Pound's *ABC of Reading* (n.d. [1934], p. 81), or in his short piece on Henry James (Pound, 1954d), which was first published in 1918 in the *Little Review*.[1]

Ian Bell (1981) traced the source of the idea behind the word *antenna* to a statement by Allan Upward, whom Pound had met at gatherings held by W. B. Yeats and whose work Pound found compatible. Bell quoted the following description of "genius" from a 1910 article by Upward.

Genius is the power of being sensitive to what is divine. The man of genius, the last delicate bud that sprouts from the tree of man, may be compared to the slender wire that rises from the receiving station to catch the unseen message that comes across the sea from an unseen continent. His duty, like the duty of the wire, is to record that message as he receives it. (Bell, 1981, p. 227)

In "The Teacher's Mission," Pound used a different analogy.

If this statement is incomprehensible and its corollaries need any explanation, let me put it that a nation's writers are the voltmeters and steam-gauges of that nation's intellectual life. They are the registering instruments, and if they falsify their reports there is no measure to the harm that they do. (Pound, 1954c, p. 58)

These gauges compare to antennae in that they "say" what a nation's intellectual life is, at the time of "registering" it, through the artist's products such as writing, painting, sculpture, or music.

An example can be taken from Pound's description of the poetry of T. S. Eliot in a 1917 essay: "His men in shirt sleeves, and his society ladies, are not a local manifestation; they are the stuff of our modern world, and true of more countries than one" (Pound, 1954b, p. 420).

Such registration (of the existing message) does not seem to entail the role of the prophet or seer of the ancient Greeks. Ernesto Grassi, in his search for Heidegerrian thought in Renaissance humanism, helps us to grasp the meaning of the poet as seer when he writes, "According to the Greek conception, a poet . . . is considered the only man who is able to order whatsoever is moving him . . . and who thus abolishes the fortuitousness, the chaos of phenomena" (1983, p. 15), that is, by giving order and form to events and things.

Albertino Mussato (b. 1261–d.1329) claimed that "the poets gave the first men the secrets of reality" (Grassi, 1983, p. 61) by going beyond the surface of particulars to the essence that is timeless. Grassi commented that this was the thesis later taken up by Giambattista Vico in his *New Science*. Grassi explained that Vico thought poetic language was primary because the poetic "characters or universals created by imagination are the 'exemplary images' or 'ideal portraits' to which we trace the individual species of beings and in which the manifold of beings comes into the open" (1983, p. 38). These "universals" are not abstractions of particular things or beings, but refer to Being (God). "In other words," noted Grassi, "Being's demands are originally shown through imagination and the image, and they urge themselves upon us through a poetic projection" (p. 39).

Inasmuch as the poet or artist can articulate the universal in beings—things and events—and inasmuch as the universal is a kind of ideal or perfection that all humans can (or ought to?) feel if not articulate, and inasmuch as we try for perfection, that artist is, in that much, a seer or prophet. This is not unlike the thesis of Robert Scholes that poetry and advertising share the characteristics of rhetoric in that they attempt to manipulate us—to appraise, evaluate, and "sell" certain specific things and attitudes (1989, pp. 111–16).

On the other hand, the artist might sense a general condition of an historical period—the period in which the artist lives—and give form to that condition. Many others also sense the condition, but the artist articulates the universality of its humanness. And inasmuch as that articulation is before any other articulation, in that much it would be a 'forerunner'—that is, a forerunner of the articulations and commentaries that would follow, but not of the 'manifestation' itself.

The concept of 'antennae' might also include the concept found in the words James Joyce gave to his character Stephen Dedalus at the end of *A Portrait of the Artist as a Young Man*, first published (serially) in 1915: "to forge in the smithy of my soul the uncreated conscience of my race" (Joyce, 1968, p. 253). "Conscience" can be read as 'the nation's intellectual life.' Did Pound appropriate the word *race* from this line? Perhaps it was used because it is a common word. McLuhan used it in his 1957 essay "Coleridge as artist" in a similar context.

But Wordsworth the seer had little sense of the auditory dimensions of language which could control great vistas of erudition and collective experience. For the auditory labyrinth is charged with the experience of the past of the race and unites the poet with history in a continuous present. (in McNamara, 1969, p. 124)

Of course, he may still here be under the influence of Pound. Again, the word *race* carried a great deal of emotional freight in the early twentieth century, after Charles Darwin and during the rise of Adolf Hitler in Germany in the 1930s.

THE NATURE OF THE ARTIST'S SENSIBILITY

John Alsberg provides an example of the artist as antenna, or conscience, in his commentary on Goya's etchings titled *Caprichos*, when he says that Goya "exposes cruelty as a basic element of civilization" (1983, p. 79). Of Goya's painting, *Madhouse*, Alsberg noted that

with this painting begins the artistic exploration of the insane, the neurotic, the hysteric. Their condition is recognized as a systematic disease of modern times . . . [and indeed] a little later Dostoyevsky, with his deep psychological insight, describes the symptoms of insanity as characteristic features of his generation. (Alsberg, 1983, p. 80)

These descriptions are similar to the one McLuhan used for the work of Edgar Allan Poe, as quoted in Chapter 4—that Poe brought morbidity into focus and gave it manageable proportions (in McNamara, 1969, p. 220). This is an equally good depiction of McLuhan's own achievement for the media of communication.

John Smith (1978) makes similar claims for Albert Camus as antenna or conscience. Commenting on *The Outsider*, which seemed to assume that life has no meaning or hope, Smith remarks on the "extraordinarily percipient discovery on the part of Camus of a condition that was growing at an alarming rate within certain types of individual in the second quarter of the twentieth century" (1978, p. 190). Notice that Smith qualifies the affected population by type and time, making this "condition" a universal from which we do not all suffer but to which we can all relate. Victorino Tejera (1965) says something similar while discussing an aspect of art as "in a sense" a remaking or reconstruction, or the "ordering" of experience.

Given the dynamics of human adaptation and of social change, the moment always comes when the art of the past no longer serves to inform current experience or the perceptions of the present. . . . These new situations requiring to be reduced to order are, in fact, often given an order, first, in art and only later in conduct or ideology. It is on these occasions, or in this sense, that art is felt to be prophetic and, hence, a revelation: it has created a new perception of the world or discovered patterns in some kinds of social and personal situations. (Tejera, 1965, p. 89)

It is important to see that this kind of prophetic act is not a prediction of what will be or what ought to be (i.e., not the artist as legislator). It is an ordering of a perception of the present as sensed by the artist's 'antennae.' It is also a qualified opinion; new situations are "often" given an order in art, and in "some" kinds of social and personal situations. One of three things could be behind this hesitation: (1) either the author is unsure and is hedging, or (2) it is really only in some situations and for some people that the statement is true, or (3) it is true only in the sense that, for any one individual at some point in life, a piece of art in any medium will have some influence on how that individual's life will be lived. Since art—by its very nature as a language of communication— can speak only to the individual (the artist and the interpreter), it is this last position that is professed here. Peter Collier has given us an appropriate quote from a letter to W. H. Auden by Louis MacNiece: "I take it that you are important and, before that, that poetry itself is important. Poets are not legislators . . . but they put facts and feelings in italics, which makes people think about them and such thinking may in the end have an outcome in action (in Collier, 1988, p. 138).

Otto Friedrich, in his biography of Glenn Gould, commented:

There was in Gould's recordings, in that detachment that could swerve into passion, in that coolness, that serenity, that ecstasy—there was a strange power unlike anything in the work of any other pianist. It was a power that made many people feel that their lives had somehow been changed, deepened, enriched. (Friedrich, quoted in Zukerman, 1989)

Thus my experience of Franz Liszt's piano concerto number two is not of some worldwide malaise or other general phenomenon, but of a musical articulation of my own personality. The response to art is personal and specific. That is, it is a personal response to a specific work. It is an artistic response in that the person "makes" that response to and with the work. It is above all an emotional response—a response to a percept, as McLuhan would have it—although, as human beings, we cannot help but have an intellectual response as well. We cannot help thinking about the work and the emotion and what these mean. The creation of that kind of response is what art does. Art that demands more than the emotional response—that requires an education, shall we say—is less than perfect. Such artwork is not so much art as a dissertation. Whatever has been the experience of the artist that has provoked the work is covered in reference to other works. Such a work cannot exact or expect an immediate response to it as a whole. For a *perception* of the effect to take place, it cannot be necessary first to "go to school." Which doesn't mean that the dissertation cannot be behind the work— but it cannot be *necessary* to the experience of the work as art.

Whenever I read the poem "Adrogué" by Jorge Luis Borges, I have to stop until I recover. There is something mysterious about the effect this poem has on me that I don't understand and don't want to understand. I want to keep and savor the wonder that it provokes. It lets "the eternal note of sadness in," as Matthew Arnold phrased it in "Dover Beach." For any artist to require that I take courses in order to appreciate any piece of art is for that artist to misunderstand the nature of the effect of a poem or a painting or a musical composition. Ezra Pound asks that we know great quantities of history and literature, and in that way his work is diminished as art. The artist as prophet or seer or teacher or communicator must create the effect by the articulation of form, thus negating the necessity to go any further than the work in hand. Otherwise the work is made less effective. This is not to say that an artist who does research into understanding a perception, or who through such mental work enables or enhances the creative process, cannot produce art that is valid, direct, and powerful.

If we have to know all that McLuhan said we must—namely, the French symbolists and James Joyce—in order to understand his message, very few would even attempt it. However, it was not McLuhan's meaning but his method that was based on the symbolists. Without completely understanding what he said, people got the message that the structures of media have effects over and above the content transmitted by them.

I must not leave this discussion without commenting on what the 'receiver' brings to the art experience. What I have said so far implies that the experience of art needs nothing more than what the average human brings to experiencing the world in general. There are those who study the arts, or one of them, and these are the people C. S. Lewis (1961) called the *cognoscenti*. Having learned much about the technique of an art and its history, their experience of a work is "impregnated with intelligence," as Lewis said (1961, p. 24). However, an artist who deliberately weighted a composition with signs and symbols known only to the cognoscenti would not be an artist, but a code maker for a secret society. Lewis's division of the world into "the few and the many" is elitist and far, far too simplified.

Serious artists create for all humanity and appeal to the emotions and the knowledge of joy, suffering, and sadness any human can experience. In no other way can art be universal and, therefore (with technical skill as a given), great.

ART FOLLOWS TECHNOLOGY

Technology—whether communication technology or not—alters a culture by changing the way things are done and talked about, and provides new objects to see and work around. What is the relationship between technology and the artist as antenna?

Claims that art can transform the conditions of life might apply to the physical aspects of life through architecture, decoration, or advertising; but making a difference in the political or economic sphere is not likely. In a study of this issue, Arthur Danto quoted William Butler Yeats: "Ireland has her madness and her weather still / For poetry makes nothing happen" (in Danto, 1986, p. 1). And W. H. Auden: "Artists and politicians would get along better at a time of crisis like the present, if the latter would only realize that the political history of the world would have been the same if not a poem had been written, not a picture painted, not a bar of music composed" (in Danto, 1986, p. 2).

Of course, such statements are hard, if not impossible, to prove. As Danto questioned, "Did jazz in any sense cause or only emblemize the moral transformations of the Jazz Age? Did the Beatles cause or only prefigure the political perturbations of the sixties?" (1986, p. 3). One might as well ask, Did McLuhan's aphorisms cause the media to increase in visibility, or did they only articulate the phenomenon? Danto's remarks on Picasso's *Guernica* indicate that art follows and does not cause events.

The painting was used as a fund-raiser for Spanish war relief, but those who paid money for the privilege of filing past it only used it as a mirror to reflect attitudes already in place, and in later years it required art-historical knowledge to know what was going on: it stood as a handsome backdrop for pickups at the Museum of Modern Art, or a place to meet a date, like the clock at the Biltmore Hotel, and it was sufficiently handsome in its grey and black harmonies to have ornamented the kitchen cupboard in a sophisticated apartment I once saw written up, where soufflées were concocted for bright and brittle guests who, no more than the hostess, realized that gutted animals and screaming mothers agonized above the formica: . . . So in the end it did about as much for the ravaged villagers as Auden's poem did for dead Yeats or as Yeats' poem did for his slaughtered patriots, making nothing relevant happen, simply memorializing, enshrining, spiritualizing, constituting a kind of cenotaph to house the fading memories. (Danto, 1986, pp. 3–4)

To succeed as a great work of art, any creation must have its effects across time and culture. If it is used at some time to promote a cause, as was the photograph *Tomoko in the Bath* by W. Eugene Smith (to protest mercury poisoning in the fish caught in Japanese waters; see Scholes, 1989, pp. 22–27), that function is temporary, even if effective. The greatness (universality) of the work rises above and goes beyond the particular event of its creation.

It is interesting that books are not counted as art in this sense. Otherwise, those "books that changed the world" could provide a counterargument. But in books it is the message (the Logos), rather than the work as art (Poiema), that acts on the mind. Here, then, it is the dissertation that matters, in both fact and fiction and including the books of Marshall McLuhan—perhaps even the tetrads. That remains to be seen in Chapter 8.

Robert Hughes devoted a whole chapter of his book, *The Shock of the New* (1980), to discussing the self-generated myth of the avant-garde artist as precursor, and the illusion that contact with works of art is morally improving. In general, Hughes says, "the history of the avant-garde up to 1930 was suffused with various, ultimately futile calls to revolutionary action and moral renewal, all formed by the belief that painting and sculpture were still the primary, dominant forms of social speech they had been eighty years before" (1980, p. 371). In actuality, the radio and newspaper had taken over. Indeed, McLuhan's insight that the mass media of communication had become dominant is what led him to explore just what their impact might be. It was the pervasiveness of black-and-white television and the first flush of TV aerials at mid-century that shot all the broadcast media into high visibility. They were becoming 'figure,' to use a McLuhan term.

The influence of radio had not been ignored. The use made of it and of loudspeakers by Hitler had been noted. McLuhan's analysis of radio as calling up group memories and fostering tribal sentiments was directly related to the Hitler phenomenon. And McLuhan once said, "On TV, Hitler wouldn't have lasted ten minutes." Of course, there is no way of proving that radio was essential to Hitler's rise. Other dictators succeeded without it. Edwyn R. Bevan (1936) was of the opinion that the English would not have been so affected.

Certainly the English are much less impressed by mere eloquence than the Latin peoples or the Germans, or even our American cousins. The extraordinary success of Hitler in Germany, won by a faculty of speech which would seem to us (to judge by the bits of his discourse heard on the wireless) energetic vociferation, would hardly have been possible in England. We are made instinctively suspicious by too sonorous or torrential eloquence. (Bevan, 1936, p. 189)

In any case, it was McLuhan who 'saw' the media as a cultural phenomenon and who tried to articulate their effects on the human enterprise, particularly with his theory that the structural impact of a medium of communication creates a sensory closure—an alteration in the balance of the senses—and this affects the way we think and act. This was McLuhan as antenna.

Perhaps it was natural that artists working fifty years on either side of the year 1900 should feel as if they ought to be creating statements about the future (although it was Beethoven who first "established and popularized the notion of the artist as universal genius" and "arbiter of public morals"; see Johnson, 1991, p. 117). These were the years that witnessed the depredations of an industrial revolution, a scientific and technological revolution, and two "revolutionary" wars, in that the nature of conducting war was radically altered and debased (if the word has any meaning in the context of killing people). Indeed, it can be argued that—rather than art foreshadowing the future—it is technology that influences or is the precursor of art. Robert Hughes (1980), after discussing the effects that looking out of the window of a moving train have on one's perception of the passing countryside, listed some of the technological and scientific changes that occurred around the turn of the century.

The first twenty-five years of the life of the archetypal modern artist, Pablo Picasso—who was born in 1881—witnessed the foundation of twentieth-century technology for peace and war alike: the recoil-operated machine gun (1882), the first synthetic fibre (1883), the Parsons steam turbine (1884), coated photographic paper (1885), the Tesla electric motor, the Kodak box camera and the Dunlop pneumatic tyre (1888), cordite (1889), the Diesel engine (1892), the Ford car (1893), the cinematograph and the gramophone disc (1894). In 1895, Roentgen discovered X-rays, Marconi invented radio telegraphy, the Lumière brothers developed the movie camera, the Russian Konstantin Tsiolkovsky first enunciated the principle of rocket drive, and Freud published his fundamental studies on hysteria. (Hughes, 1980, p. 15)

The whole point of Alsberg's book was to show that culture, especially recently, does not occur in a vacuum but in "the complex fullness of a technological civilization" (and therefore "art trends are not self-determined"), and that the material foundations of a culture are "not only evident in the subject matter and content of art, but also in its very substance: the artistic form" (1983, p. 2).

McLuhan would support that view through his basic theory that the dominant medium of communication fundamentally effects changes in our psyches, and in our social and political acts (even in the altered form I present herein). In his essay on "Coleridge as Artist," McLuhan wrote that "Newton's *Optics* established a correspondence between inner and outer worlds, between the forms and textures of the world and the faculties of perception and intellection, which has affected the practice of every poet and painter since his time" (in McNamara, 1969, p. 118). Again, in "The Aesthetic Moment in Landscape Poetry," written in 1951, he noted that "Mallarmé had been led to this technique by an aesthetic analysis of the modern newspaper," which also "stands . . . behind *Ulysses*" (McLuhan, 1969, p. 158).

THE SERIOUS ARTIST AS OLDER AND WISER THAN EVERYONE ELSE

McLuhan referred to Wyndham Lewis's explanation of the role of the artist: "The artist is older than the fish. The artist goes back to the fish. The few centuries that separate him from the savage are a mere flea-bite to the distance his memory must stretch if it is to strike the fundamental slime of creation" (Lewis, 1971, p. 257). But Lewis was prone to pump himself up with such claims. In Geoffrey Wagner's biography of Lewis we find a concatenation of them: "Deprived of art . . . Life instantly becomes so brutalized as to be mechanical"; "Only artistic life, the life of the intelligence, is true life. The only reality exists in the artist's intellect" (Wagner, 1957, p. 106). It is a small step from this to the wishful boast of the American artist George Bellows cited by Robert Goldwater and Mario Treves (1947).

The ideal artist is he who knows everything, feels everything, experiences everything, and retains his experience in a spirit of wonder and feeds upon it with creative lust. He is therefore best able to select and order the components best suited to fulfill any given desire. The ideal artist is the superman. (Goldwater and Treves, 1947, p. 461)

It is fortunate that Bellows qualified that frightening vision by inserting the word *ideal*. T. S. Eliot brings us back from these exaggerations when he writes, "Hyperbolically one might say that the poet is *older* than other human beings" (1933, p. 155); and he does so by using the adjective *hyperbolically* to recognize that this sort of talk *is* an exaggeration.

Maurice Beebe (writing prior to our awareness of sexual prejudice in language) came closer to the artist's reality when he said,

Just as every artist is a man, every man is to some extent an artist, a maker of things, and the alienation of the artist is not unlike that of many men in a world where the center does not hold and where even the crowd is a lonely one. To try to create something out of chaos, if only by cultivating our gardens, is to heed the lesson of the artist. (Beebe, 1964, p. 313)

In this sense, any act of making something—anything—is an artistic act, but perhaps not a "serious" or professional artistic act. Indeed, if we were not all sensitive as the artist is sensitive, there would be no art. The appreciation of art—simply as "liking" a specific painting or poem and relating to it emotionally—is absolutely necessary if there is to be art at all. Without an audience that is sensitive to art (is artistic), art would die. But all that I am saying is that human nature comprises the element of being artistic.

In *From Cliché to Archetype* (McLuhan and Watson, 1970), not only is the *artist* described as an "ordinary, familiar person" because the techniques of art are familiar ones, but also "every man today is in this sense an artist—the administrator, the scientist, the doctor, as well as the man who uses paint and sculpts stone" (p. 119). And, I would add with Beebe, the common ordinary gardener. Marshall McLuhan and Wilfred Watson are here trying to say that preliterate people and people in the electric age are different from people who lived in the age of print—the Middle Ages, the Renaissance, and up to the nineteenth century. The artist in the Renaissance used processes with which ordinary folk were unfamiliar, we are told; but in the electric age, everyone uses the "natural processes of rhythms" of "modern electric technologies" that "require such timing and precision that only the following of processes in nature can be tolerated" (p. 119). This murky verbiage points us to the properties of acoustic space, in which space all people (not just artists) are involved—and involved in "making, creating; exploring, revealing" (Nevitt, 1967, p. 15). Considering the discussion of these characteristics in Chapter 6, I conclude that any "making" of any kind by anyone in any time is, to some degree, art.

What the professional artist has that other individuals do not have is skill—with words, pencil, paint, stone, or whatever medium is chosen—a skill and a sensitivity to the medium as an expressive device, as a mode of communication. Alsberg knew that all perception by any person—"artistic or non-artistic—is giving structure to sensory experiences" (1983, p. 23). What distinguishes the artist's perception is that the sensory experience is given form. It becomes a "visual conception" (p. 23), or an aural or tactile one.

There is a nice example of the ordinariness of the artistic sensibility being parlayed into the priestly function in McLuhan's essay on "Coleridge as Artist" (in McNamara, 1969). In a somewhat involved correlation of Isaac Newton's *Optics* with the use of external landscape—in both its visual and auditory aspects—as the 'language' of Nature, we are given the instance of Samuel Coleridge in the role of "pontifex or bridger" between Nature (as a language) and the mind. That is, Coleridge used a natural environment—its sights and sounds—to get across an idea. The excerpt is from Coleridge's poem "France: An Ode," a discussion about Coleridge's personal reaction to the French Revolution and the principle of liberty. The excerpted lines are from the conclusion, which tells us that it was on the edge of the sea, with the wind and the waves murmuring together, that the poet "felt" liberty. (Note that the last line is not given in McLuhan's essay.)

> —on that sea-cliff's verge,
> Whose pines, scarce travelled by the breeze above,
> Had made one murmur with the distant surge!
> Yes, while I stood and gazed, my temples bare,
> And shot my being through earth, sea, and air,
> Possessing all things with intensest love,
> O Liberty! my spirit felt thee there.
>   (Coleridge, 1836 [1797], pp. 131–32)

McLuhan's commentary was as follows:

The poet is here exercising his priestly powers of purifying the wells of existence, exerting his primary imagination which is the agent of all perception, not the secondary imagination which brings art into existence as an echo of the functions of perception.

The world felt as Aeolian harp and as an apocalyptic language, on one hand, and the poet as pontifex or magus, on the other, pretty well sets the stage for all the problems of aesthetics from Thomson, Collins, and Akenside to Coleridge, Keats, and Shelley. These problems, moreover, remain our own. For the work of Yeats, Joyce, and Eliot represents a continuous development of poetic theory and practice along these lines. The artist becomes scientist, hierophant, and sage, as well as the unacknowledged legislator of the world. (in McNamara, 1969, p. 120)

There is a lot happening in these few sentences. First, the meaning of 'pontifex' as bridger has picked up its secondary meaning of a 'member of the council of priests in ancient Rome,' which is reinforced by adding 'magus' (a member of a hereditary priestly class among the ancient Medes and Persians, with overtones of 'magician'). To that is added Shelley's term *hierophant*, the chief priest of the Eleusinian mysteries, with overtones of expositor or advocate.

Second, there is the surprising conclusion, which seems to be the result of the poet's "purifying the wells of experience" by being a bridge between external nature and ideas. Strangely—as if the exaggeration were not his—McLuhan continued, "Naturally enough, accompanying this hypertrophy of the artistic role in society has come a good deal of bewildered dissent" (in McNamara, 1969, p. 120).

It seems to me that McLuhan's remarks on the primary and secondary imaginations are a reversal of the work of the professional artist. I refer to the act of the artist's being to give form, structure, or order to perceptions. Most if not all humans, when standing on the edge of a cliff, feeling the wind in their hair, and hearing the surge of waves, would be imbued with feelings similar to those of Coleridge. Expansive views make the spirit soar. It is the artist's skill to take these same perceptions and form them into words or pictures or sounds that convey the feeling of freedom and liberty—the feeling that any individual has, but that few individuals can express in such a way as to make their fellows feel those perceptions again. It is not that artists *purify* the wells of experience, but—considering wells as storage tanks—artists *make* them (thus making perceptions manifest). They make the storage tank (the work of art), not the contents (the experience). The experience is there for all, but not all of us can make just the right storage device that will hold the essence of the experience to be 'made' by the receiver, to be reexperienced again and again through all time.

THE ARTIST AS ANTENNA BUT NEITHER PROPHET NOR LEGISLATOR: SHELLEY AND TROTSKY

When Stephen Dedalus used the phrase *conscience of my race*, we can read into 'conscience,' in this context, more than sensitivity. It carries the connotation of guide, guardian, angel, scold—Percy Bysshe Shelley's 'legislator.' T. S. Eliot called Shelley's claim an exaggeration (Eliot, 1933, p. 25), and there is evidence that Shelley himself would agree. In the summary of the unwritten second part of Shelley's "A Defence of Poetry," we are told that it was to have applied the principles of the first part to "the present state of the cultivation of poetry" and to have been a "defence of the attempt to idealize the modern forms of manners and opinions, and compel them into a subordination to the imaginative and creative faculty" (Shelley, 1976 [1821], p. 69). This seems to mean that poetry is closely allied with the awakening of a people to achieve a "beneficial change in opinion or institution" (p. 70), and this alliance ("herald, companion, and follower") leads to the final sentence: "Poets are the unacknowledged legislators of the world" (p. 71).

However, if Shelley had pursued this point, it seems clear he would have contradicted himself. After saying that in earlier epochs poets were called "legislators" or "prophets" and that "a poet essentially comprises

and unites both these characters" (Shelley, 1976 [1821], p. 22), Shelley
went on to clarify what he meant:

Not that I assert poets to be prophets in the gross sense of the word, or that
they can foretell the form as surely as they foreknow the spirit of events: such
is the pretence of superstition, which would make poetry an attribute of prophecy, rather than prophecy an attribute of poetry. (Shelley, 1976 [1821], p. 23)

He then described the act of the poet as the identification of universals:
"A poet participates in the eternal, the infinite, and the one; as far as
relates to his conception, time and place and number are not" (Shelley,
1976 [1821], p. 23). This is exactly the point made in the discussion above
of Coleridge's "France: An Ode," with the qualification that while everyone participates in the eternal, the infinite, the one, it is the artist who
identifies or articulates the experience. Shelley's strongest statement
against the poet as legislator is this: "A poet therefore would do ill to
embody his own conceptions of right and wrong, which are usually
those of his place and time, in his practical creations, which participate
in neither" (p. 33). He emphasized this position by giving an example:
"Those in whom the poetic faculty, though great, is less intense, as
Euripides, Lucan, Tasso, Spenser, have frequently affected a moral aim,
and the effect of their poetry is diminished in exact proportion to the
degree in which they compel us to advert to this purpose" (p. 33). A
contemporary example is Ezra Pound, whose political and economic
opinions cause his work to suffer this diminishment (McGann, 1988).
     Leon Trotsky made the mistake of seeing the artist as communicator
of a "moral aim."

Our policy in art, during a transitional period, can and must be to help the
various groups and schools of art which have come over to the Revolution, and
to allow them complete freedom of self-determination in the field of art, after
putting before them the categorical standard of being for or against the Revolution. (Trotsky, 1960 [1924], p. 14)

Trotsky understood that the artist must be free to determine what art
will be, yet he also declared that "the new art will be realistic. The
Revolution cannot live together with mysticism. Nor can the Revolution
live together with romanticism" (Trotsky, 1960 [1924], p. 236). In discussing the Eiffel Tower, he asked disparagingly, "What is it for? . . . At
present, as everyone knows, the Eiffel Tower serves as a radio station.
This gives it meaning, and makes it aesthetically more unified" (p. 247).
Art must have a purpose. But then, there are two kinds of art: "the
works whose themes reflect the Revolution, and the works which are
not connected with the Revolution in theme, but are thoroughly imbued

with it, and are coloured by the new consciousness arising out of the Revolution" (p. 228).

Here are Shelley's poet as legislator and poet as participator in the universal. Comparing stories and poetry, Shelley wrote:

The one is partial, and applies only to a definite period of time, and a certain combination of events which can never again recur; the other is the universal, and contains within itself the germ of a relation to whatever motives or actions have a place in the possible varieties of human nature. (Shelley, 1976 [1821], p. 28)

It is this universal aspect that is at the heart of Trotsky's touching example of a work "coloured by the new consciousness."

But when the young poet, Tikhonov, without writing about the Revolution, writes about a little grocery store (he seems to be shy about writing of the Revolution), he perceives and reproduces its inertia and immobility with such fresh and passionate power as only a poet created by the dynamics of a new epoch can do. (Trotsky, 1960 [1924], p. 228)

Trotsky confiscates this artist to the cause.

In discussing an early version of this chapter—when it was a separate paper—an anonymous reader wondered if the artist's perceptual experience could be *combined* with moral and political insight. He (or she) aptly pointed out that there are four options open in the process of expressing ideas about the world: (1) emphasis on perceptual experience; (2) stress on explanation; (3) insistence on moral conception, and the ideal; or (4) description of actual events in the form of reports or happenings. Any and all of these programs are possible for the artist, but the danger of deliberately combining moral and political insight with perceptual (artistic) experience is clear from both Shelley's and Trotsky's analysis.

MCLUHAN'S FIGURE/GROUND MODEL RELATED TO ART

In the introduction to *Laws*, we read that the work of the artist is to report on the current status of 'ground' by exploring those "forms of sensibility" made available by each new mode of culture (p. 5). What is meant by this claim? What is the ground the artist examines before reporting on it? We are told that the ground of any human artifact is not only the situation that gives rise to it, but all the services and disservices that accompany it (p. 5). For example, the automobile is 'figure' and roads, service stations, suppliers of oil and parts, and parking lots are 'ground'—until the roads or parking lots become a problem, and then they can become figure. The automobile as figure excited our attention, creating or bringing with it a service environment that remained more or less unnoticed. Unnoticed, that is, until the highway became so overwhelming that it loomed as figure and then efforts had to be bent to solving the problems created by such land-devouring services as freeways and parking lots.

McLuhan, of course, exaggerated the invisibility of ground, saying that its study is "virtually impossible"—but that it is, on the other hand, the "normal activity" of artists (*Laws*, p. 5). In fact, most people are aware of service environments of this kind—even people who are not artists. They might not be able to articulate or make a statement about how this environment fits in with everything else. But that is what artists do. They can express, in some medium, the 'feelings'—and in that way the meanings—of new forms in a culture, as well as new meanings felt in old forms.

However, it wasn't just the background of services and the experience itself that needed articulation. It is the tremendous number of figures being produced throughout the industrial/technological world, such as automobiles, railroad engines, railroad stations, and large cities. As Hughes said, "The master-image of painting was no longer landscape but the metropolis. In the country, things grow; but the essence of manufactures, of the city, is process, and this could only be expressed by metaphors of linkage, relativity, interconnectedness" (1980, p. 12). The last three words translate into McLuhanese as 'acoustic space,' 'tactility,' 'interval'; but here it is not electricity that is the (psychic?) 'cause,' but the processes of manufacturing and of getting from one place to another in a large city.

Note that Hughes calls the terms "metaphors." He did not reify them. He did not say we are living in interconnected space, as McLuhan said we are living in acoustic space. We need to realize that Marshall Mc-Luhan was a poet and that when he made such statements he was speaking metaphorically. If he had called himself a "poet" and what he said "poetry," people would have understood him, or would have been not so confused and frustrated by his method as they were, thinking he was speaking as a scholar and therefore talking "factually."

In the *Laws* passage about the ground of a technology or artifact, we are told, in parentheses, that the environment is the 'medium' (p. 5). We are told that these environmental "side effects" are a new form of culture, and the phrase used to clarify or define that opinion is the famous 'the medium is the message.' But *Laws* is a book that calls any human artifact a 'medium' (a metaphor). Thus, both figure and ground are included in the term *medium*. Indeed, there is one sentence that conveys in a commonsense way the nature of the figure–ground relationship: "All situations comprise an area of attention (figure) and an area of inattention (ground)" (p. 5). This is perfectly clear and needs no pronouncement that the study of the area of inattention is "virtually impossible." Of course it's possible. People haven't got the time, or just aren't interested in making a scientific investigation or painting a picture—even if they could, even if they were artists.

McLuhan recognized the pioneering 'figure/ground' work of Edgar Rubin, but broadened the meaning of the concept to cover the organization of consciousness and perception (*Laws*, p. 5). In an analysis of Rubin's research, John M. Kennedy commented on Rubin's attitude toward the issue of attention/inattention: "It may be that Rubin played down the role of attention a little too much. It may be there is more to attending than a change in the direction of attention. It may be that hints and instructions can control markedly different ways of looking" (1973, pp. 99–100). Kennedy's interpretation of Rubin was that "the differences between figure and ground cannot be explained by differences in the direction of attention" (p. 99)—although Rubin (1958 [c. 1915] had noted that conscious intent can also play an important role.

The 'figure/ground' research is mainly concerned with pictorial representations. McLuhan used the concept as a model of attention/inattention to technological devices: the device, as novelty, receiving the attention; the services necessary to maintain the device receiving, normally and by most people, little or no attention. On the other hand, the content of a communication medium would get the attention, while the medium as a technological device affecting or shaping the content would not. McLuhan's purpose was to get us to attend to that aspect of the medium.

So when we learn that "a great poet or serious artist should be able to perceive or distinguish more clearly than ordinary men the forms and objects within the range of ordinary experience" (*Laws*, p. 5), we can expect those artists to be saying something about the ground or service areas backing up some artifact of primary attention, or about experiences that come with new mechanical or electric forms of, for example, travel or communication. We ordinary people experience ground subliminally, according to McLuhan, but we are not aware or interested because our attention is on the machine or the content of the medium. This is perfectly normal. However, the quotation from Eliot about Dante that McLuhan used to illustrate the artist's sensitivity to areas of inattention (*Laws*, pp. 5–6) was not really about such an act by Dante, but was about Dante's ability—regardless of whether he was dealing with figure or ground—to *express* a wider range of emotions than other people. In that quotation from Eliot's *To Criticize the Critic* (1965), we see that Eliot, too, thinks the great poet should be able to "perceive and distinguish more clearly than other men, the colours or sounds within the range of ordinary vision and hearing" (p. 134). It would be hard to prove that artists perceive colors or sounds more clearly than ordinary men (and women), and even harder to define what is meant by 'ordinary men.' Eliot also says that the great poet—not any other kind—"should perceive vibrations beyond the range of ordinary men" (p. 134).

But we are entering here the territory of the artist as 'superman,' and since "vibrations" are unspecified in Eliot's pronouncement, they can be made to mean anything—even those areas of inattention surrounding the motor car. I think we would do better to leave this myth alone about great poets and serious artists, and reduce their function to the expression and forming of the feelings we get from common (and uncommon) human experiences. As Herbert Read wrote:

That man is unhappy, indeed, who in all his life has had no glimpse of perfection; who in the ecstasy of love, or in the delight of contemplation, has never been able to say: It is attained. Such moments of inspiration are the source of the arts, which have no higher function than to renew them. (Read, 1948, pp. 83–84)

Was Marshall McLuhan such an artist? I shall now explore that possibility.

NOTE

1. I have to thank Carol Roberts, then of the Reference Department of the University of Western Ontario's Weldon Library, for tracking down the source of the phrase *antennae of the race*.

8

Marshall McLuhan as Artist

INNIS—MCLUHAN

McLuhan definitely saw himself as an artist, and his style a "serious art form." He would disagree with Herbert Read's 'art as renewal' concept (Read, 1948). In talking to Gerald Stearn, he said of those who held to this narrow definition, "They are talking about art as a blood bank, as stored precious moments of experience. The idea that art's job is to *explore* experience too never dawned on them" (in Stearn, 1967, p. 285). James Curtis thought McLuhan had combined two of Henri Bergson's statements about art: "that the artist tears the veil from reality, and that laughter counteracts rigidity" (Curtis, 1978, p. 85). Two comments can be made on this. One is that the act of tearing usually contains or implies a moral position, and it was this aspect of McLuhan's explorations—the fact of his forceful "why can't everyone see what I see" style—that led people to think he was in favor of the new communication technologies, when he felt exactly the other way.

The second comment is about laughter loosening rigidity. McLuhan's puns and jokes were notorious. In his introduction to a reprint of Harold Innis's *Bias of Communication* (1951), McLuhan makes sure that Innis's humor does not go unnoticed: "There is one department in which Innis never fails, and in which the flavour of Inniscence is never lost—his humour. Humour is of the essence of his aphoristic association of incongruities" (McLuhan, 1964a, p. xiv). He then gives an example of Innis's humor: "Referring to the neglect of the horse as a factor in military history, he recalls that 'E. J. Dillon remarked concerning a mounted policeman that he was always surprised by the look of intelligence on the horse's face' " (p. xiv).

This observation is not as important for understanding Innis as it is for understanding McLuhan. In this introduction, McLuhan was really talking about himself. He began by saying that Innis used the same kind of "contemporary awareness" as did poets and painters since Baudelaire and Cézanne: "Without having studied modern art and poetry, he yet discovered how to arrange his insights in patterns that nearly resemble the art forms of our time" (McLuhan, 1964a, p. vii). This art form was "a mosaic structure of seemingly unrelated and disproportioned sentences and aphorisms" (p. vii). This is actually a description of McLuhan's own "multi-level prose." McLuhan then proceeded to give us an example from Innis: "How exciting it was," wrote McLuhan, "to encounter a writer whose every phrase invited prolonged meditation and exploration: 'Alexandria broke the link between science and philosophy. The library was an imperial instrument to offset the influence of Egyptian priesthood' " (p. ix). McLuhan's comment on these two sentences was that they implied and invited "an awareness of the specific structural forms of science and philosophy as well as of the structural nature and functions of empires, libraries, and priesthoods" (p. ix). Donald Theall's (1971) analysis of one of McLuhan's sentences makes a fascinating comparison of styles. First is the McLuhan sentence, then Theall's commentary.

"Heidegger surfboards along on the electronic wave as triumphantly as Descartes rode the mechanical wave." . . . Here there is not only the metaphor itself employing a covert analogy, but also an explicit analogy in which Descartes' relation to his age and its mode is similar to Heidegger's relation to his age and its mode. The point of the analogy is an exposé of the inadequacies of Descartes for an electric age. Whether we agree with McLuhan's facility or not, the technique when it is successful provides a poetic discovery. (Theall, 1971, p. 13)

MALLARMÉ—MCLUHAN

In 1953, McLuhan wrote a paper on "Joyce, Mallarmé, and the Press" (in McNamara, 1969). Here we can find a good description of McLuhan's artistry. "It was Mallarmé," McLuhan wrote, "who formulated the lessons of the press as a guide for the new impersonal poetry of suggestion and implication" (in McNamara, 1969, p. 11). This is the idea of the poem as probe. Stéphane Mallarmé's task "had become not self-expression but the release of life in things" (p. 11). In opposition to Herbert Read's concept of poetry as 'renewal of moments of inspiration,' this was poetry all set to tear the veil from reality. Although the artist (no different from anyone else) cannot help but express some of the self, the intent of the art process is to release life, to discover—but to do so in such a way that the reader must be part of the process. So McLuhan could say of Innis as artist that "Innis takes much time to read on his own terms" (McLuhan, 1964a, p. ix). Of himself, McLuhan said, "I expect my readers to do more work than I did. But I'm offering them opportunities, roles of initiative" (in Stearn, 1967, p. 287). He then related this position to that of T. S. Eliot.

When people approached T. S. Eliot and said, "Mr. Eliot when you were writing 'Sweeney among the Nightingales' in that passage XYZ did you mean . . ." he would wait patiently and say, "Yes, I must have meant that, if that's what you got out of it." Now Eliot was saying that the reader was co-poet. The reader's job was to make poems. Not to get his essence but to make a poem with the ingredients handed to him. (in Stearn, 1967, p. 287)

McLuhan related all of this to his own method: "That's the way I feel about critical responses. Many of the meanings people get—insofar as they are related to media—are not the ones I had in mind but they might serve very well as exploratory devices" (in Stearn, 1967, p. 288). The conclusion I come to, therefore, is that the form of McLuhan's tetrads contains the ingredients of insight into human artifacts. And since the tetrads are 'art' (under McLuhan's definition), it is therefore legitimate to say that the perceptions manifested by this form will give rise to several quite different tetrads (or poems), and the question as to which is the right one is meaningless.

In "Joyce, Mallarmé, and the Press," McLuhan went on to say of Mallarmé (and of himself), "The job of the artist is not to sign but to read signatures. Existence must speak for itself. The artist has merely to reveal, not to forge the signatures of existence. But he can only put these in order by discovering the orchestral analogies in things themselves" (in McNamara, 1969, p. 15). For McLuhan, these "orchestral analogies" were the laws of media—the grammar of the effects of human artifacts. This was "the impersonal art of juxtaposition" (p. 16), in which the artist takes no moral stand. (McLuhan said he was "goofed" by that when he wrote The Mechanical Bride—McLuhan, 1951; see McLuhan, 1957). So, having set up the juxtaposition in the tetrads, the artist has nothing more to do. If we see McLuhan's Understanding Media (1964b) and The Gutenberg Galaxy (1962) as extrapolations of the tetrads, in order to return to the poems themselves we must leave all that McLuhan wrote and said and must simply contemplate the "ingredients" of the tetrads alone. The other works are a gloss on this final creation.

As McLuhan said of Mallarmé, the juxtaposition of observations enables "each reader to be an artist" (in McNamara, 1969, p. 16). In the tetrads, this juxtaposition of observations would include the aphorisms and quotations and the structural components themselves. Quoting Mallarmé, McLuhan wrote, "It is the rhyming and orchestrating of things themselves which releases the maximum intelligibility and attunes the ears of men once more to the music of the spheres" (p. 16). Then McLuhan quoted from John Ruskin's *Modern Painters*, in which the "discontinuous picturesque techniques in medieval and modern art" were described under the term *grotesque* (p. 17). It is a perfect description of McLuhan's art form.

A fine grotesque is the expression, in a moment, by a series of symbols thrown together in bold and fearless connection of truths which it would have taken a long time to express in any verbal way, and of which the connection is left for the beholder to work out for himself, the gaps, left or overleaped by the haste of the imagination, forming the grotesque character. (in McNamara, 1969, p. 17)

A tetrad is a grotesque. Not those structured as lists of effects as in Marshall McLuhan and Bruce Powers (1989, pp. 169–78), but as they are displayed across the pages in *Laws of Media* (see Figures 4.1 and 4.2). As such, the tetrad is an art form that is the start of a conversation. It is imperative to say that "the gaps . . . left . . . by the haste of the imagination" are Soren Kierkegaard's "individual problems," cited in Chapter 3, hurrying by one another because the "scientific" call to order was not given (Kierkegaard, 1944, p. 9). But neither Mallarmé nor McLuhan nor any artist is a scientist.

We need only compare the description of Ruskin's grotesque with Toby Goldberg's concatenative description of McLuhan's writing style to see the mosaic and the grotesque come together.

By bringing together on a single page, glossy headlines, ideas, facts, foreign phrases, theories, metaphors, analogies, quotations, the jargon of science and art, puns, and other esoteric data, and by circular reasoning, literary name-dropping, juxtaposition, phrasemaking, excessive explanations at one moment and glaring gaps in information the next, he offers a kaleidoscope of observations that attempts to simulate the workings of the human mind. (Goldberg, 1971, pp. 320–21)

And, it is important to add, to *stimulate* the human mind.

Donald Theall's remark, in the most literary of the critiques of McLuhan, becomes significant at this point: "The thesis that McLuhan is fundamentally an artist, a poet manqué, is complicated by the fact that if he is an artist he has created a new form, or at least contributed to bringing a new form to fuller development" (1971, p. 239). Theall was thinking of concrete poetry, the *essai concrète*, as the new art form—one that mimicked the newspaper page. Nothing could be more apt as a description of the tetrad structure.

IF AN ARTIST, WAS HE A POET?

If the tetrads are "a series of symbols thrown together in bold and fearless connection of truths" (in McNamara, 1969, p. 17), so are the aphorisms such as 'the medium is the message,' 'the global village,' and 'the omnipresent ear and moving eye' (radio and television). If these are not statements of *the* truth, as most people heard them they are statements of *a* truth—of part of the truth about media no one had noticed before.

In this final section, I intend to examine the question of whether or not McLuhan was a poet beyond the 'grotesque' artistry of Ruskin and the tetrads. McLuhan fulfilled the criterion he so often cited in *Laws* about the artist's being aware of the changing nature of society and acting as an 'antenna.' He made his 'reports' in rhythmic, original, and metaphoric language, insisting that he never had concepts, only 'percepts.' His constant denial that, in his *public* works, he was for or against any medium or state of culture proclaimed the objective stance of the artist who, ideally, stays away from moral and political insights. "Don't get steamed up about moral implications," he once said to me in a letter. "I was goofed by that line in the *Bride*. What is needed is cool study of media dynamics" (McLuhan, 1957). Nine years later McLuhan was still insisting that "I'm not for tactile and against visual, any more than the man who shouts 'FIRE!' is in favour of incendiaries. I don't explain, I explore" (quoted in Howard, 1966, p. 99).

John Sturrock (1989) wrote in his review of *Laws of Media:* "It was largely thanks to McLuhan that the electronic media forever lost their innocence, and that we began looking beyond their manifest content to the previously disregarded implications for the way we act and think of the media." In McLuhanese, the 'ground' of the media (the content being the 'figure') was explored and reported, and in a style that was more memorable and with lines more quoted than most, if not all, other contemporary poets.

The following "McLuhanisms" were set together by Richard Pollak.

- The hullabaloo Madison Avenue creates couldn't condition a mouse.

- Most executives ride high, wide and handsome because they have joined certain new technologies. Eliza Doolittle is certainly in this category. *My Fair Lady* is really a massive parable of the ordinary success of the twentieth century in technology.

- The whole educational system is about to do a great flip-over from instruction to discovery, with the students as researchers.

- We haven't a clue in our technology as to how to turn it off. We don't know where it came from.

- All that has ever appeared on the retinal screen of mankind over the centuries is old movies.
- The teach-in is purely student participation in the process of discovery in which the teacher, if anybody, is to be brainwashed.
- On TV, Hitler wouldn't have lasted ten minutes, and if it weren't for the hot media the war in Vietnam would be over in an hour. (Pollak, 1966, pp. 56–57)

It is not difficult to pile up examples of this kind. They can be analyzed for alliteration, rhythm, and literary devices such as metaphor and hyperbole.

Percy Bysshe Shelley, in his *A Defence of Poetry*, wrote, "Plato was essentially a poet—the truth and splendour of his imagery, and the melody of his language, are the most intense that it is possible to conceive" (1976 [1821], p. 26). I have questioned the accuracy of McLuhan's 'facts'; but perhaps, in a grotesque, such accuracy is not the point. One can also question the 'truth' of McLuhan's imagery (by saying, e.g., that Hitler would have used TV as he used radio); McLuhan's failing here was in the ambivalence of his vision of himself, of his own role. As an academic, he often scorned academia. In a letter, he once wrote, "How can people manage to pretend that scholarship exists to advance knowledge? This is (not) only not true, but never has been true" (in Molinaro, McLuhan, and Toye, 1987, p. 450).

At the same time, he thought that the artist has to live in messy circumstances "in order to keep his senses in play" (in Molinaro, McLuhan, and Toye, 1987, p. 339). The ambivalence is evident in the purpose of the book *Laws of Media*: the desire to be scientific, to be able to prove his theories, to be able to have his probes made replicable so his insights could be used by anyone for the good of society. On the other hand, as Pollak reported, " 'Marshall,' says a former colleague, 'claims he's a scientist. I've never agreed with that, I think he's a poet. You can't argue with him, just as you can't argue with Tennyson or Browning' " (1966, p. 57). Goldberg quoted David Myers's view of the form of McLuhan's art: "The form of McLuhan's poetry is talk—fragmentary, mischievous talk. Inevitably it breaks down under particular scrutiny" (in Goldberg, 1971, p. 325). McLuhan confirmed this, in his dialog with Gerald Stearn, when discussing what critics said of his own work: "When critics say, 'One gets a lot of misconceptions and misunderstandings from these pages,' they're being naïve. Not to understand the media of discourse is naïve" (in Stearn, 1967, p. 288). Discourse is the verbal interchange of ideas; but as an artist, McLuhan was less interested in changing and interchanging than in creating ideas for others to discuss.

When we read that David Myers said, "Attempts to subdue McLuhan to some sort of coherence are doomed to failure" (quoted in Goldberg, 1971, p. 325), we need to think about C. Day Lewis's remarks on the enjoyment of poetry: "('Poems are made with words, not with ideas,' said a great French poet), don't rack your brains over sense. A line here, an image there, will catch your fancy. It is a clue, a starting point" (1956, p. 9)—like a *DEW-LINE* aphorism.

Shelley noted, regarding what can be counted as poetry, that "the parts of a composition may be poetical, without the composition as a whole being a poem. A single sentence may be considered as a whole, though it may be found in the midst of unassimilated portions: a single word even may be a spark of inextinguishable thought" (1976 [1821], pp. 28–29). Ben Jonson, writing in the seventeenth century, was of the same opinion: "A poem is not alone any work or composition of the poet's in many or few verses: but even one alone verse sometimes makes a perfect poem" (1946, p. 136). He then gave an inscription by Aeneas as an example: *"Aeneas haec de Danais victoribus arma"* (Aeneas consecrates these arms won from the conquering Greeks). And a line from Martial: *"Pauper videri Cinna vult, et est pauper"* (Cinna wishes to seem a pauper, and is a pauper). Speaking of the ancient oracles, Jonson said, "Whatever sentence was expressed, were it much or little, it was called an Epic, Dramatic, Lyric, Elegiac, or Epigrammatic poem" (p. 136). McLuhan's aphorisms can certainly be classed as epigrammatic, and it is significant that he was known as the "media guru"—the oracle of the New Communications" (Pollak, 1966, p. 56).

Not all would agree with Lewis and Shelley and Jonson, and one who might not is Francis Turner Palgrave, whose collection of verse McLuhan carried on a walking tour of England in 1932. In the preface to the first edition in 1861, Palgrave wrote, "A few good lines do not make a good poem" (1964, p. x). Of course, he did not say that those few good lines were not poetry. One must also keep in mind what Ben Jonson said of poets or writers who produce great numbers of verses without much work: "I have met many of these rattles that made a noise and buzzed. They had their hum, and no more. Indeed, things wrote with labour deserve to be so read, and will last their age" (1946, p. 137). McLuhan produced his sayings with seeming ease, although many years of refining were behind them. The concepts were hinted at in his literary essays and in his articles for the journal called *Explorations*, published through the mid–1950s. In my analysis of McLuhan's media charts (Neill, 1973a, p. 280; reprinted here as Appendix II), I showed the progression of ideas and the refinement of language with respect to McLuhan's basic insights. The clearest early statements occur in "Culture without Literacy" (McLuhan, 1953), his first article in *Explorations*. Even *The Mechanical Bride* (McLuhan, 1951) did not make such obvious pronouncements, probably because it was written before McLuhan felt the influence of

H. A. Innis, whose *Bias of Communication* (1951) was published the same year as the *Bride*. It was Innis's work that brought a focus to McLuhan's interest in the effects of technology on writers such as Mallarmé and Joyce. His own exploration of these effects was McLuhan's scholarly contribution, but Innis and, for example, Walter Ong (1982) were more "scientific"; McLuhan was more "poetic." To show just how firm the basic McLuhan tenets were in the fall of 1953, I shall match quotations from that first article in *Explorations* with quotes from the *Report on Project in Understanding New Media*, written in 1960.

World Information Flow

"Today the entire globe has a unity in point of mutual information awareness which exceeds in rapidity the former flow of information in a small city" (McLuhan, 1953, p. 118).
"Today it is axiomatic that we live in a global space fed by information from every point on the sphere at the same time" (McLuhan, 1960a, p. 9).

Medium and Message

"But the fury for change is in the form and not the message of the new media" (McLuhan, 1953, p. 123).
The medium becomes the message" (McLuhan, 1960a, p. 19).

Object Language

"But in respect of this anonymity, it is necessary to regard not only words and metaphors as mass media but buildings and cities as well" (McLuhan, 1953, p. 125).
"We are obliged to learn the language of objects, and especially of those objects that are media" (McLuhan, 1960a, p. 13).

Perhaps much of what McLuhan said won't last, but he gave the language new words to describe the effects of media, not the least of which are 'the medium is the message' and 'the global village.' As Jonson would put it, these "will last their age."

In the introduction to *The Interior Landscape* (a collection of McLuhan's literary criticism), McLuhan confessed to a youthful devotion to Romantic Poetry: "In the summer of 1932 I walked and hiked through most of England carrying a copy of Palgrave's *Golden Treasury*. There had never been any doubt in my mind that art and poetry were an indictment of human insentience past and present" (in McNamara, 1969). He spent much of his life trying to wake people from their somnambulism and "insentience" where media were concerned.

But it is significant that McLuhan also wrote in that introduction, "When my critics imagine I am being vaguely metaphorical, I, too, am trying to be literal and precise" (in McNamara, 1969, p. xiv)—as he had just said of James Joyce. Again the ambiguity of role: the poet (being metaphorical) or the scholar (literal and precise).

Early in the nineteenth century, Shelley observed:

All authors of revolutions in opinion are not only necessarily poets as they are inventors, nor even as their words unveil the permanent analogy of things by images which participate in the life of truth; but as their periods are harmonious and rhythmical, and contain in themselves the elements of verse; being the echo of the eternal music. (Shelley, 1976 [1821], p. 27)

Uniquely, in his time, Marshall McLuhan was attuned to that music.

Appendix I

McLuhan Remembered: A Personal Memoir

After reading Barry Powe's (1984) article on his experience in McLuhan's course "Media and Society" in 1978, I realized how different was my time in the same course ten years before. I had accepted a position as associate professor at the University of Western Ontario in 1967 in the new School of Library and Information Science and was under some pressure to acquire a graduate degree of some kind, since SLIS was a graduate school. I began an M.Ed. at the Ontario Institute for Studies in Education in 1968, part-time, and signed up for McLuhan's Course 1000 in September 1969.

The class met Tuesday evenings at 8:00. If there were twelve members enrolled in the class it was hard to tell, for the room in the Coach House where it was held was always crowded. There were nineteen folding metal chairs and it was necessary to arrive early to get one, which I did, since I found it extremely uncomfortable to sit on the floor with no room to stretch. On any night there could be forty or fifty people in the room, all ages and all kinds, including one young woman with flowing black hair and long loose garments. She might have come straight in from the desert of Omar Khayyám.

McLuhan, whom I had known casually for many years, passed out his famous reading list and introduced Harley Parker, the artist. The first two classes were conducted by Parker, showing the slides that were the illustrations for *Through the Vanishing Point* (McLuhan, 1968a).

Parker, like Barrington Nevitt, a later co-worker with McLuhan, spoke just as McLuhan did—broad generalizations in pontifical tones with a twinkle in the eyes and a smile just beginning at the corners of the mouth. There was no doubt about the 'truth.'

Each of the regular students was required to present a paper for discussion. It was during the discussion of one of the early ones that I discovered a side of McLuhan I had not expected. After Marshall had made some comment about the reasons Eskimos built igloos, a student who had been in the Arctic attempted to provide some facts that might be helpful in bringing McLuhan to a more accurate version of the case. McLuhan, with a sudden change of tone, lifted his head, although he was standing, and said icily, "Don't criticize my work until you understand it." I was shocked. This was suddenly not the friendly open professor I had known as an undergrad, nor the questioning mind I had experienced through correspondence in the late 1950s.

Still, the moment passed and did not return. There was only one other incident of a similar nature, which occurred a year or two later. I had decided to take my children to meet McLuhan, and took one or two at a time on the train to the Tuesday night classes. They were still the open meetings I had known in 1969–70. I had my ten-year-old son with me the night the student's presentation was held in the theater in the Forestry Research Building on Spadina Avenue. The subject was a discussion of Bob Dylan's music, and the student's presentation was in the form of a film that showed an interview and discussion interspersed with songs by Bob Dylan. After about ten minutes, McLuhan stood up and said, "Stop the film. This is boring. If that's all that's going to happen we've seen enough." A desultory discussion ensued, but did not last long.

While my son did not get a close look at McLuhan in the scurry of the large auditorium, I saw McLuhan playing the teacher as impresario. Or what I saw was McLuhan living his slogan *the medium is the message*. The content of the filmed discussion was not what he perceived as important. He saw four discussants discussing—for ten long minutes—and no action, no visuals. The medium was being incorrectly used, and he had responded emotionally to the abnormality.

I wonder if I am being overly charitable? I gather that McLuhan was not always the easiest person to get along with. I don't know. Perhaps this "temper" was a residue of the operation to remove a brain tumor in 1968. Philip Marchand reported that there was an increase in McLuhan's sensitivity for years afterward (1989, pp. 214, 231). My relationship with him was always warm and friendly. I had taken one of my first-year courses from him in 1946–47. It was called "Seven Shakespeares," and all I remember was some reference to Hamlet, Johnny Ray, and Frank Sinatra. During the next four years, while I was studying history, he was going around campus giving a slide lecture that would become *The Mechanical Bride* (McLuhan, 1951).

After I graduated from the University of Toronto Library School in 1951, I went to work in the Long Branch Public Library. Long Branch was on the far reaches of what would become Metro Toronto and was then one and a half hours by streetcar from Saint Michael's College (at the University of Toronto). I sat in on McLuhan's course on modern poetry during 1951–52. It was very enjoyable, and one could make references and comparisons to current popular culture such as advertisements and comics.

It was after one of these classes that Marshall invited me home for supper. We stopped first at the Baybloor for a beer, then took a streetcar to 27 Wells Hill Avenue. His wife Corinne was not expecting anyone and had to set another place at the table. I have always been easy around little children, and it was just as well, for all six of the McLuhan brood were still very young. You can imagine the hectic time Mrs. M. was having if you have ever been in a large family of small children. I sensed the difficulty, ate, bided my time, and said farewell. Not before, however, I had been shown one—or was it two?—small paintings by Wyndham Lewis.

Strangely, the next time I was in his home was when I was in the process of taking my own children to his classes. I came in one night to find the class cancelled. Marshall was not well. Not wanting to disappoint the two kids I had with me, I took a bold chance and phoned and asked if I could come and see him. He was (or was it Corinne?) most obliging.

When we arrived at 3 Wychwood Park, we were taken into the basement, which was not at all finished. There was McLuhan watching television, and Eric was working away at some wiring. We watched *To Catch a Thief*, McLuhan commenting on the blue of the sea in the film. When this episode was finished, I gathered my children and left. McLuhan said good-bye at the door. It was one of those glowing golden nights after rain. The house seemed sheltered in an umbrella of leaves shot through with magic as they caught the light from the doorway. The pond in the hollow was hidden in shadows.

The first time I had been in McLuhan's house was when he lived at 10 Elmsley Place on the campus of Saint Michael's College. It was when he was working on the second issue of *Explorations*. I had been down to the Ryerson Press to purchase books for the Long Branch Library and had seen an unusual publication. It was a large book, like a scrapbook, made up of simulated newspaper pages from different periods of history—something like this: "Rome. Today Julius Caesar invaded Gaul." It was my intention to tell McLuhan about this, since I knew he would be interested.

Corinne and the children were not to be seen. Indeed, when I went in the door, no one was to be seen. I called, and McLuhan said he'd be right down. I went into the living room, but only by moving books was I able to find room on the sofa to sit. I was not there long. This was an issue of *Explorations* he was doing by himself, he said, and he was overwhelmed trying to meet a deadline. He was interested in the news-paper book and said, "I must get a copy." He went and phoned Ryerson immediately. We talked about Malcolm Ross's *Our Sense of Identity*, which quickly became *Our Sense of Idensity*, and *Our Sense of Our Density*. And then I left.

Once, in the 1970s—I don't remember when—I was in Toronto for some reason and dropped in at the Coach House. McLuhan was dictating to his secretary, Mrs. Stewart. He was standing in the small entrance foyer that led into the larger meeting room, which was decorated with posters and a large painting by René Cera.

He interrupted himself and took me upstairs to his office for a chat. There was a couch or narrow bed and one chair. On the floor were piles of books—perhaps ten piles of two to four books each. These were the chapters of something he was working on. "The way to write a book today," he said, "is to get yourself some file folders, fill them with relevant clippings, and then comment on them." His comments, at that stage of his career, were made conversationally to Mrs. Stewart. The result of the file-folder method was *From Cliché to Archetype* (McLuhan and Watson, 1970), the mosaic idea in practice, with the chapters in alphabetical order.

Course 1000, "Media and Society," ended with an examination that asked us to make up six questions arising from our reading of one of the books on the reading list. The bulk of our grade was based on the papers we had presented and, I imagine, our contribution to the dis-cussions. None of this regular academic sort of information was ever presented to us.

We had the experience one evening of talking by the light of a single 60 watt bulb in a floor lamp placed on the table, no other lamp being available. McLuhan had been told that discussion improved under such conditions. He did not continue the practice.

Some people felt he was opinionated. Others were turned off by his style of pontificating. I had known him long enough not to let it bother me. A reviewer in the *New York Times* once said of him, "He makes a habit of saying somebody like Plato, Kant, Einstein, Toynbee, Spengler, Mumford, 'failed to grasp' what he grasps so easily" (Cort, 1966). But McLuhan, like most philosophers who are truly philosophical, knew that he was, after all, a man, and I have always assumed that he was thinking of himself as much as of every other famous person when he wrote in *Explorations*, "For it has always been an advantage to have direct contact with eminent men, if only because proof positive of their essential mediocrity spurs younger talent" (1955, p. 56). He knew he had the broadcast media by the tail, and he knew why and how he had them by the tail, and he enjoyed it enormously.

As a matter of fact, that statement by McLuhan reinforced my own attitude toward the famous and powerful, which I had figured out for myself as a teenager. I have warmed myself by it many times.

McLuhan once said, "Man should maintain a constant, nonstop dialogue with his creator. And for that kind of dialogue you don't need even to be verbal, let alone grammatical." Sometime during the night of the last day of 1980, Marshall McLuhan was called to a personal face-to-face dialogue with his Creator, leaving many still wondering what "McLuhanism" was all about. Was it the media madness of the 1960s happenings? Was it the eclectic phrasemaking guru? No. If anything, it was the poet-philosopher's cry to "be aware," to look without bias, without prejudice, without taking hard-and-fast positions (unless for the sake of argument), at what's really going on out there in the world of communication and culture.

Appendix II

McLuhan's Media Charts Related to the Process of Communication

Marshall McLuhan's media charts were published in a supplement to *AV Communication Review* (AVCR) in 1960 (McLuhan, 1960b). An updated version of a selection of these charts by Barrington Nevitt (1967), an associate of McLuhan, was included in a relatively obscure journal (not indexed by any of the major indexing services) in 1967. The original charts are the bulk of McLuhan's *Report on Project in Understanding New Media* which is available, it seems, only through the U.S. Office of Education (McLuhan, 1960a). These charts are fundamental to McLuhan's operational terminology of 'low definition,' 'high definition,' 'structural impact,' and 'sensory closure' (or 'subjective completion'), but the articles and books about McLuhan do not mention them. Even Donald Theall (1971), in the most intensive and scholarly critique of McLuhan to date, has for some reason ignored the media charts, although he lists the *Report on Project in Understanding New Media* in his bibliography.

Because these charts are fundamental to any understanding of Mc-Luhan's approach to media effects, it seems to me that much more attention should be paid to them, even though their psychological validity can be questioned. I use the word *questioned* advisedly; for in spite of the evidence McLuhan provides, it is open to investigation whether our psychological patterns and sensory preferences are influenced as strongly as McLuhan has said they are by the structure of the media—and this factor is the key to McLuhan's media and society opus.

It is in the structure of the chart's process that he shows how the specific sense impact of a medium elicits the effort of the other, or "opposite," senses to maintain sensory balance. As he said in that early report:

Chiasmus is indispensable to understanding media since all information flow by feedback—that is by its effects—operates simultaneously in opposite modes. But until I worked out the charts it was impossible to show this to anybody. This was because we still rely on pictorial modes even in the non-visual electronic age. (McLuhan, 1960a, p. 23)

This one quotation raises a number of questions: whether chiasmus is directly comparable to feedback; whether feedback from the consequences of an "information flow" (I am thinking in terms of David Berlo's 'interpreter' model of the communication process; see Ball and Byrnes, 1960) is an "opposite mode" to the stimulus, or a different mode; whether "mode" carries the meaning intended; and whether, assuming that electric information movement creates 'acoustic space,' we really do live in a nonvisual world, considering the continuing hold of the textbook and print on our education system. I do not intend to examine these questions. My purpose is to analyze the structure of McLuhan's media charts in an effort to understand exactly how they work in his terms and on his terms. He himself was not interested in categorizing the effects of the media into abstract classifications as I attempt to do. To have done so would have inhibited the power of the chart process as an investigatory tool that he could use, knowing as he does that such labeling would immediately freeze the model into unreality. This essay, therefore, takes the chart structure one step further in its development as a conceptual model. The next step would be to test the hypotheses on which the charts are based.

CONTEXT IN WHICH CHARTS WERE DEVELOPED

Before looking at the charts, however, it might be valuable to set them briefly in the context of McLuhan's thought and of the Title VII, NDEA[1] project during which they were developed. To begin with, McLuhan's key operating principles were in evidence long before 1960. He seems to have stated his conclusions before developing, except in a cursory way, any arguments to prove them. That is, he saw that the media had effects on society, but it was not until he worked out the charts that he was really able to explain why they had the effects they did. This personal procedure of working backward from effects to causes is consistent with his study of poetic effects and the detective story analogy: "If we can establish what happened, it is often unnecessary to explain why it happened" (McLuhan, 1969, pp. 158–59). This seems to be a guiding principle in the McLuhan approach. One is left to presume either that why it happened is unimportant, or that the reasons will become obvious. It must be recognized that there is some support for this approach in the psychology of interpersonal communication. Paul Watzlawick, Janet Helmick Beavin, and Don D. Jackson, of the Mental Research Institute in Palo Alto, California, discuss this particular point.

> While there can be no doubt that behavior is at least partly determined by previous experience, the search for causes in the past is notoriously unreliable. ... [Memory is not only based] mainly on subjective evidence and, therefore, liable to suffer from the same distortion the exploration is supposed to eliminate, but whatever person A reports about his past to person B is inseparably linked to and determined by the ongoing relationship between these two persons. If, on the other hand, the communication between the individual and the significant others in his life are observed directly ... patterns of communication can be eventually identified that are diagnostically important and permit the planning of the most appropriate strategy of therapeutic intervention. This approach, then, is the search for pattern in the here and now rather than for symbolic meaning, past causes, or motivation.
>
> If seen in this light, the possible or hypothetical causes of behavior assume a secondary importance, but the effect of the behavior emerges as a criterion of prime significance in the interaction of closely related individuals. (Watzlawick, Beavin, and Jackson, 1967, pp. 44–45)

This method of investigation is directly analogous to McLuhan's perceptions of the method of studying the relationship between individuals and the communicating environment. His method has remained constant over the years.

Although it is possible to find adumbrations of McLuhan's perceptions in his literary studies in the late 1940s and early 1950s—particularly those on James Joyce, whose writings, along with the works of T. S. Eliot, were partly instrumental in arousing or steering McLuhan's interest into the area of popular culture—the clearest statements occur in 1953 in "Culture without Literacy" (McLuhan, 1953), his first article for the periodical *Explorations*. Even *The Mechanical Bride* (McLuhan, 1951) does not make such obvious pronouncements, and this is probably because it was written before McLuhan felt the influence of H. A. Innis, whose *Bias of Communication* (1951) was published the same year as the *Bride*. To show just how firm the basic McLuhan tenets were in the fall of 1953, I am going to match quotations from that *Explorations* article with quotes from the *Report on Project in Understanding New Media*, written in 1960.

World Information Flow

> "Today the entire globe has a unity in point of mutual information awareness which exceeds in rapidity the former flow of information in a small city" (McLuhan, 1953, p. 118).

"Today it is axiomatic that we live in a global space fed by information from every point on the sphere at the same time" (McLuhan, 1960a, p. 9).

Medium and Message

"But the fury for change is in the form and not the message of the new media" (McLuhan, 1953, p. 123).
"The medium becomes the message" (McLuhan, 1960a, p. 19).

Object Language

"But in respect of this anonymity, it is necessary to regard not only words and metaphors as mass media but buildings and cities as well" (McLuhan, 1953, p. 125).
"We are obliged to learn the language of objects, and especially of those objects that are media (McLuhan, 1960a, p. 13).

Writing

"Writing creates that inner dialogue or dialectic, that psychic withdrawal which makes possible the reflexive analysis of thought via the stasis of the audible made spatial. Writing is the translation of the audible into the spatial as reading is the reverse of this reciprocal process. And the complex shuttling of eye, ear and speech factors once engaged in this ballet necessarily reshape the entire communal life, both inner and outer, creating not only the 'stream of consciousness' rediscovered by contemporary art, but ensuring multiple impedimenta to the activities of perception and recall' (McLuhan, 1953, p. 119).
"The phonetic alphabet alone, of all forms of writing, translates the audible and tactile into the visible and abstract. Letters, the language of civilization, have the power of translating all of our senses into visual and pictorial space" (McLuhan, 1960a, p. 5).

Evidence of McLuhan's great concern for human values—often over-looked (Neill, 1971)—is also present in that early article: "How many thousands of years of change can we afford every ten years? May not a spot of culture-lag here and there in the great time-flux prove to be a kind of social and psychological oasis" (McLuhan, 1953, p. 119). In the 1960 *Report*, McLuhan suggests one method of attaining "culture lag" for preserving social and psychological balance: "We may be forced, in the interests of human equilibrium, to suppress various media as radio or movies for long periods of time, or until the social organism is in a state to sustain such violent lopsided stimulus" (1960a, p. 9).

With this background, we see that Marshall McLuhan began his Title VII, NDEA project with most of his ideas already developed. It was his discovery "early in 1960" that "the sensory impression proffered by a medium . . . was not the sensory effect obtained" (McLuhan, 1960a,

p. 1), plus the need to state his insights as "testable hypotheses," that led to the creation of the charts, probably in February of that year. These charts and their hypotheses were then the substance of a presentation at the U.S. National Education Association, Department of Audio Visual Instruction, or DAVI (now the Association for Educational Communications and Technology, AECT), conference the first week of March 1960. Having worked one month on these charts, and given an explanation of them at the conference, McLuhan does not seem to have returned to them for further elaboration. We must therefore begin with his DAVI explanation as the "definitive" statement.

HYPOTHESES UNDERLYING THE CHARTS

The first hypothesis underlying the charts says that the structural impact of a medium is incomplete, insofar as the human senses are concerned, in all media except speech. That is, all man-made (technological) media—from writing to TV—lack several of the major human senses. TV, according to McLuhan, incorporates all but taste and odor, and in this way brings a sensory balance closer to the equilibrium of the unaided human communication process.

The second hypothesis is that the sensory completion tends to occur for those senses omitted in the structural impact. The best example of this, at least for those who grew up with the radio programs of the 1930s and 1940s, is the strong visualization of the characters in the stories on the air—even to the point of looking into the back of the radio to see if little people were performing there. This hypothesis is the basis for the generalization that "all information flow . . . operates simultaneously in opposite modes" (McLuhan, 1960a, p. 23).

The third hypothesis directly relevant to the chart system is that low definition (LD) of the sense image[2] in the structural impact of a medium results in corresponding intensity of the sensory closure for that particular image. McLuhan gives an example: "For instance, LD, in causing much effort of completion in telephone and TV, greatly weakens the visual fill-in for telephone and the tactual-kinesthetic fill-in for TV" (1960b, p. 82). The low definition (LD) nature of telephone conversations (e.g., unstructured sentences and paragraphs) results in low definition of visual fill-in—as opposed to the high definition of radio sound and scripts, and the corresponding intensity of visual "completion" or closure.

The clearest explanation McLuhan gives of the process outlined in the charts is as follows:

Any high definition (HD) structural impact (SI) tends to yield an intense subjective completion (SC) sensuously with strong overflow into the low definition (LD) area of psychic repetition of the SC pattern.

Low definition (LD) structural impact (SI) tends to give the subjective completion (SC) the role of reinforcing the structural impact (SI) with resulting overflow into the high definition (HD) area of psychic repetition of pattern. (McLuhan, 1960b, p. 81)

The operating principle expressed is that for any high definition of information the receiver's participation is low, and for any low definition stimulus the receiver's participation is high. Herein lies the view of the TV age as participatory, involved, and process oriented in sensory and intellectual preferences (the psychic response to TV and radio as communication media). Similarly, print is seen as having a different effect: separating, objectifying, and emphasizing the critical approach from an individualized point of view.

Difficulties begin to arise when these hypotheses are seen together. For one thing, there is a slight conflict between the hypothesis that the sensory completion tends to occur for those senses omitted in the sensory impact—an hypothesis presented without qualification—and the hypothesis that for a low definition sense impact the fill-in in sensory completion is for the senses of the image, not the omitted senses. Admittedly, the LD sense impact omits much or some of the possible sensory resolution, but it can be asked, What *of* the senses omitted? Are they not also involved in the completion process? Or is the fill-in activity overriding, as in the example that the effort at completion in telephone communication "greatly weakens the visual fill-in"? This seems a reasonable explanation, but then the first hypothesis needs to be qualified to say that 'SC tends to occur for those senses omitted in SI, when the SI is in HD.'

A second difficulty arises when the explanations are matched to the charts. Radio, with a high definition audio impact, has an intense visual sensory completion. By definition, this should show up in the low definition corner of the chart as a "psychic repetition" of the visual pattern. In the 1960 AVCR "Radio" chart (see Figure A.1), the LD corner contains the words *Hit Parade / Group memories / distant drums, / horns, / tribal / sentiments*. Some of these are audio descriptors; and as descriptive of psychic effects, "*Hit Parade*," "distant drums," and "horns" leave much to be desired.

The statement that the low definition image in TV "greatly weakens ... the tactual-kinesthetic fill-in for TV" does not seem to jibe with the explanation that "whether in respect to its low definition, retinal impression, or its high tactility, the television image elicits a very strong participant response from the viewer" (McLuhan, 1960b, p. 82). In the first the fill-in is greatly weakened, and in the second there is a strong response. There should be a corresponding intensity of SC for an LD sense image, including kinesthetic and tactile in the case of television, accord-

Figure A.1
McLuhan's "Radio" and "Television" Charts (1960b) Compared with Nevitt's "B&W TV" Chart (1967) Based on McLuhan

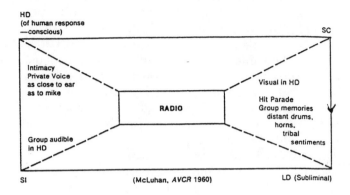

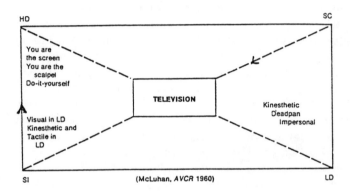

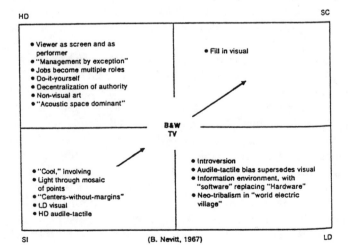

ing to the chart. There is further confusion when one looks at the AVCR "Television" chart (again see Figure A.1) where this low definition kinesthetic impact appears in the low definition corner, although the operating principle told us that a low definition impact is reinforced in the sensory completion "with resulting overflow into the high definition (HD) area." Yet the other senses indicated on the chart appear (as the arrow shows) to flow into the high definition—or "conscious"—corner, where the three phrases *You are / the screen / You are the / scalpel / Do-it-yourself* imply participation and "tactual" involvement.

An understanding of the TV chart's elements is made more difficult when the interpretation given by Barrington Nevitt is considered (see Figure A.1). Nevitt, director of innovations at the Ontario Development Corporation, worked closely with McLuhan, attending the "Media and Society" seminars that are Course 1000 at the University of Toronto. Nevitt's charts are a reworking of the originals to make them more representative of the process. His "B&W TV" chart has the audible–tactile impact as high definition, in opposition to McLuhan's earlier chart. HD tactility does correspond, however, to McLuhan's statement, previously quoted, regarding TV's "high tactility" (McLuhan, 1960b, p. 82). Nevitt then follows the principle that an HD impact ends up in the LD corner of psychic responses. But according to McLuhan's explanation, there is a "strong overflow into the low definition (LD) area of psychic *repetition* of the SC pattern" (p. 81, my emphasis). Nevitt's chart indicates that the SC pattern is a visual filling-in. Therefore one would expect the repetition of this visual pattern to appear in the LD area of the chart—not an "audile–tactile bias."

Nevitt further complicates matters by departing from McLuhan's initial chart in the *Report on Project in Understanding New Media*—where the SC is described as "maximal participation via all senses" (McLuhan, 1960a, p. 137)—and also, for some reason, altering the form of the chart itself, so that the lines of flow are cut off by vertical and horizontal divisions.

These difficulties are intensified when we compare McLuhan's "Print" chart with that of Nevitt (see Figure A.2). The HD visual sense impact of print is completed (SC) in McLuhan's chart (noted in the *Report* text at p. 55,[3] but not on the chart itself) by the filling-in of the omitted senses: "audile—tactile." McLuhan indicates this completion as low definition; yet the operating principle is that any HD impact "tends to yield an intense subjective completion," presumably of the omitted senses. Nevitt's "Printing" chart, on the other hand, has the SC intensifying the visual—although his text tells us that, "when the definition of a visual sensory input increases, the subjective nonvisual response also increases, nonlinearly: it becomes tactile through sensory closure" (Nevitt, 1967, p. 21). Is his chart or his text to be followed?[4] If the charts are

Figure A.2
McLuhan's "Print" Chart (1960a) Compared with Nevitt's "Printing" Chart (1967)

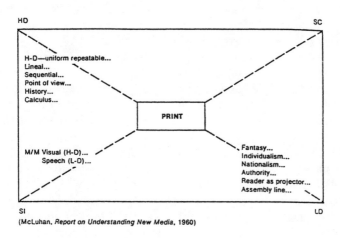

(McLuhan, *Report on Understanding New Media*, 1960)

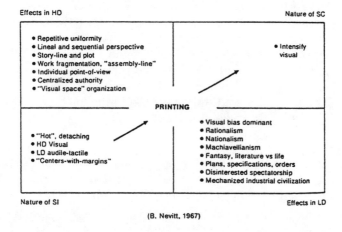

(B. Nevitt, 1967)

supposed to be useful in learning the effects of the media with any predictable soundness and reliability, then some consistency must be attainable.

A PATTERN FOR PREDICTING THE EFFECTS OF THE MEDIUM

Having identified this problem of visual/acoustic inconsistency, let me leave it momentarily. I will, at least tentatively, resolve it when I present my own interpretation of the chart process. There is another, more important problem in using these charts as they are. The psychic pattern produced by the form of the medium tells us, according to McLuhan, what the effects of the medium will be in our individual and social lives. These effects are shown in the LD and HD areas of the chart. The question is, Can we define the nature of these areas in such a way as to be able to use them confidently?

We can begin by noting that the LD corner has been labeled "subliminal," the HD corner as "conscious" (see Figure A.1). "Subliminal" was a much used word in the late 1950s, as in "subliminal advertising"; and McLuhan does not define his use of it. By reading through the chart descriptions in the *Report*, some light is thrown on the meaning intended.

One characteristic of the H-D corner of the chart of any medium is that it tends to be occupied by conscience [sic] individualist traits while the L-D corner tends to get filled in with unconscious collectivist traits. (McLuhan, 1960a, p. 95)

In another place we read this: "In the LD corner we find, as always, the less obvious and less conscious components of the medium as a 'system' " (p. 103). The high definition effects are described as "obvious": "In the HD corner of this, as of any medium, one tries to note the most obvious characteristics" (p. 113). And again: "in the HD corner of obvious and conscious effects" (p. 112).

A second element in defining the HD and LD corners is the use of the labels *individualist* and *collectivist*. Generally, the charts for prints, telegraph, telephone, radio, and phonograph place individualist traits in the HD effects area, and the collectivist in the LD area. For example, the description of the telephone chart says,

In the LD corner we find, as always, the less obvious and less conscious components of the medium as a "system." Among our sensory responses, the tactile and kinetic, perhaps some visualization? But especially all the social and collective effects of the telephone. (McLuhan, 1960a, pp. 103–4)

There is still, however, no consistency. In the graphic charts, McLuhan puts the tactile components in the HD corner, then says in the text, "The tactile sensations are probably Low Definition (L-D) at best as compared with eye and ear" (p. 64). And in that same section he states, "It is not necessary for all observers to be agreed on the SC (or the HD–LD for that matter) of a given image or medium" (p. 64). In the description of the press chart, we find this statement: "The HD–LD diagonal tends to represent the social or collective effects of a structured image on society" (p. 77). The place of the individualist traits seems to be eliminated, but he later says, "So on our HD–LD diagonal we find, unexpectedly, the collective in the HD corner, and the private in the LD or subliminal corner" (p. 77). For the print chart (see Figure A.2), the social effects are in the HD corner and the individualist traits in the LD corner, with the definiteness of this indicated by the phrase *as always*.

In terms of social effects, the HD modes of print create uniformity, repeatability, lineality, individualism, and "point of view." The LD effects here as always are relatively subliminal: for the individual, a rich "inner" life of dreams and fantasy. Habits of inner drive, inner direction, and self-set objectives or fixed points of view are only a few of the galaxy of effects of print on readers. (McLuhan, 1960a, pp. 55–56)

There is no pattern indicating that media with HD sense impact will have the effects on the individual in the HD corner and the effects on the collective group, or society, in the LD corner. Nor is there a discernible pattern to indicate that all electric media have the same placement of effects. The print chart, which is describing a nonelectric and high definition medium, has habits of inner drive and inner direction in the LD corner; and yet TV—an electric and low definition medium—also has its effects for individuals in the LD corner. McLuhan's question "On the other hand what about Low Definition (LD) with regard to television?" results in the conclusion "Does this not suggest that the viewer is in an extremely introverted role?" (p. 135). The HD effects of TV are established very inadequately: "Let us ask again what is the most notable and popularly recognized feature of television?" The answer seems to be opposed to the individual-viewer response of the LD effects: "Perhaps it is the negative charge that it is the enemy of reading" (p. 135). LD effects seem here to be the inner response; HD effects, the response in society.

Looking again at the charts, however, it seems that the application of any pattern is impossible. McLuhan says in the text that the social effects of HD modes of print are "uniformity, repeatability, lineality, individualism, and 'point of view' " (pp. 55–56). Three of these effects he places in the HD corner of the chart (see Figure A.2), but individualism is in the LD corner. It can be argued that individualism is an inner effect, but why then call it a social effect? On the other hand, nationalism would normally be classed as social, and it is listed in the LD corner along with "a rich 'inner' life of dreams and fantasy" (pp. 55–56).

Nevitt's printing chart (see Figure A.2) puts "Centralized authority" and the "assembly-line" in the HD effects, while McLuhan has them among the LD effects. Nevitt makes a neat distinction in one instance, identifying a sensory effect rather than the examples of individual and social organization "caused" by the change of sensory preferences resulting from media impact. In his printing chart, he notes among the LD effects that the visual bias is dominant. Among the HD effects he lists " 'visual space' organization." In his TV chart (see Figure A.1), Nevitt makes the same differentiation. The "audile—tactile bias" is in the LD corner (the inner sensory response), the comparable HD effect of the multisense impact of TV is "acoustic space dominant." These effects seem to place the sensory response, as an "inner" and individual preference, in the LD effects area, and the spatial or organizational preferences for the "outer" world—the individual's interaction with other people and with things—in the area of HD effects. This split would support McLuhan's hesitant positioning of inner and outer effects in his description of the impact of the TV image.

There is reason to believe, from an analysis of the text, that the TV chart was the first one drawn, although it appears last in the *Report*. Perhaps McLuhan's initial intuition was correct and his later placing of "collective" effects in the LD corner was simply a part of the developmental process. At one point, for instance, after discussing the effects in HD and LD, he writes, "I had no such plan in mind to begin with, but was simply groping my way" (p. 95). Even in the introduction, which seems to have been written after all the charts were complete, he says, "What I'm trying to do in these charts and in the questions and suggestions that go with them is to discover the dynamic symmetries and contours of the media. There is no point in being apologetic since the entire effort is experimental" (p. 27). It would appear that, as he became more familiar with his HD/LD terminology (i.e., he stops writing the terms in full and also stops using a hyphen between the initials, as in "H-D" for high definition) and surer in his understanding of the process, he returned—in the charts for the press, writing, and print— to placing individual inner and cultural effects in the LD sector, and social structural or organizational effects in the HD sector.

ELEMENTS AND EFFECTS OF MCLUHAN'S CHART SYSTEM

With this reasoning in mind, therefore, I have attempted to identify and categorize the various elements and effects associated with the chart system. In this, my purpose is to clarify the fundamental base of McLuhan's thinking and to present the chart model as a potential tool for anyone to use in media study. It is well to point out again that I am assuming the validity of McLuhan's hypotheses. It is apparent that, until the chart model is made conceptually clear, there is little chance of making valid tests of the assumptions behind it.

Of the four broad areas of the model, the most difficult to define is the subjective completion or sensory closure element. In all but the most extreme of cases (exemplified in the movies *The Ipcress File*, where hypnosis is induced by bombardment with sound, and *The Mind Benders*, where hallucination is induced by total sensory deprivation), the human psyche maintains a degree of sensory balance. If McLuhan's thesis is correct, that the psychic filling-in of omitted senses creates "effects" in our sensory preferences, then the effects of print would logically be to move the individual to auditory–tactile values and attitudes. His conclusion is that "print man" is strongly biased visually. Indeed, there is little doubt that the sensory effects of the media are caused not so much by closure as by their structural impact: the fragmentation of the age of print relating to the fragmenting of sounds and words into hard metallic type, and the "sensory wholeness" of the TV age relating to the electric speed of information transfer orally and pictorially. These two different effects are epitomized in the concepts of 'visual space' and 'acoustic space.' These are the "world view" poles between which civilizations swing. According to McLuhan, the sensory impact of the dominant communication medium pushes the society in one direction or the other, creating a bias that is reflected in cultural preferences and in the organizational structuring of human association and action.

That the structural impact/sensory closure process might not be sense fill-in only, however, is suggested by a comment made by McLuhan twelve years after the *Report on Project in Understanding New Media*, when he stated that it seemed as if the main perception of Henry James was what McLuhan calls "SI/SC"—that what we take in does not correspond with "actual experience," but that a "transformation" takes place of all "input and intake."[5] This matches an earlier opinion in *War and Peace in the Global Village*.

Literate man easily imagines that there is a direct correspondence between the input and the experience. He lives in a world of correspondences and matchings and repetitions which he calls rationality and science. Until fairly recently any set-up was scientific if it could be exactly reproduced or repeated. This, of course, can never happen in any moment of human experience. Every input is totally transformed. (McLuhan, 1968b, p. 141)

It makes one wonder if the early SI/SC process has not changed to become a model of the kind of idiosyncratic structuring of knowledge that David P. Ausubel identified:

On the one hand, the psychological structure of knowledge is a derivative of subject matter content abstracted from the logical structure of knowledge, and the psychological meaning is an idiosyncratic elaboration of logical meaning; on the other hand, the logical structure of knowledge is a topically systematized reorganization of the psychological structure of knowledge as it exists in mature scholars in a particular discipline. (Ausubel, 1964, p. 226)

McLuhan's concepts of 'matching' and 'making' are relevant here. Matching is the scientific method of replicating or repeating experiments exactly. Making, or discovering and exploring, is the mode of inquiry of the acoustic bias. McLuhan equates 'making' with the idiosyncratic structuring of percepts and concepts in the mind of each individual. Another way of putting this was discovered by McLuhan: "I am using a new perception (new for me) . . . [i.e.,] the user is the content of any medium" (1972c). He repeats this view of sensory closure in a letter to the Toronto *Globe and Mail* in which he makes the following statements: "The meaning, or content, is somewhat different for each of us. . . . When people share the same experience, each creates a totally different meaning for that experience merely by relating it to his own unique being" (McLuhan, 1972a).[6] This makes SI/SC a little easier to understand. One can use a tradition that begins at least as far back as 1511 when Erasmus wrote, "After all, it is what a reader brings to a passage rather than what he finds there which is the real source of mischief" (1961, p. 176).

However, the key to McLuhan's predictive apparatus is the perception of 'space.' In a 1972 handout paper, he says of one of his "new perceptions" that "still puzzles me," "It concerns the North American space syndrome, which I have never found verbalized anywhere. We go outside to be alone and we go inside to be with people. This pattern is antithetic not only to the European but to all other cultures whatever" (McLuhan, 1972c).

In their *Variations in Value Orientations*, F. R. Kluckholn and F. L. Strodtbeck also recognize the space problem.

A sixth common human problem which is considered to be necessary to the value-orientation scheme is that of man's conception of space and his place in it. Unfortunately this problem and the ranges of variability in it have not been worked out sufficiently well to be included at the present time. (Kluckholn and Strodtbeck, 1961, p. 10 fn.)

The problem of identifying conceptions of space, both visual and acoustic, is too large a one to be attempted here, as well. It is possible, however—if one accepts McLuhan's position at face value, as I am doing at this time—to use his definitions and examples. This will allow the development of a model of his media charts that is, if not what he would have come to, at least an outgrowth from the seeds he planted. McLuhan treats visual and acoustic space characteristics almost as opposites. A summary of these characteristics is provided by Nevitt (1967, table 1), and I have relied heavily on the list of "metaphors and probes" that Nevitt associates with the "visual and acoustic space models" (see Chapter 6). In my chart (see Figure A.3),[7] the characteristics of the two spaces (visual and acoustic) are divided by a slash in the HD and LD corners.

The 'structural impact' flows to the SC corner, but I have included

Figure A.3
Chart Identifying and Categorizing Elements and Effects of McLuhan's Media Charts

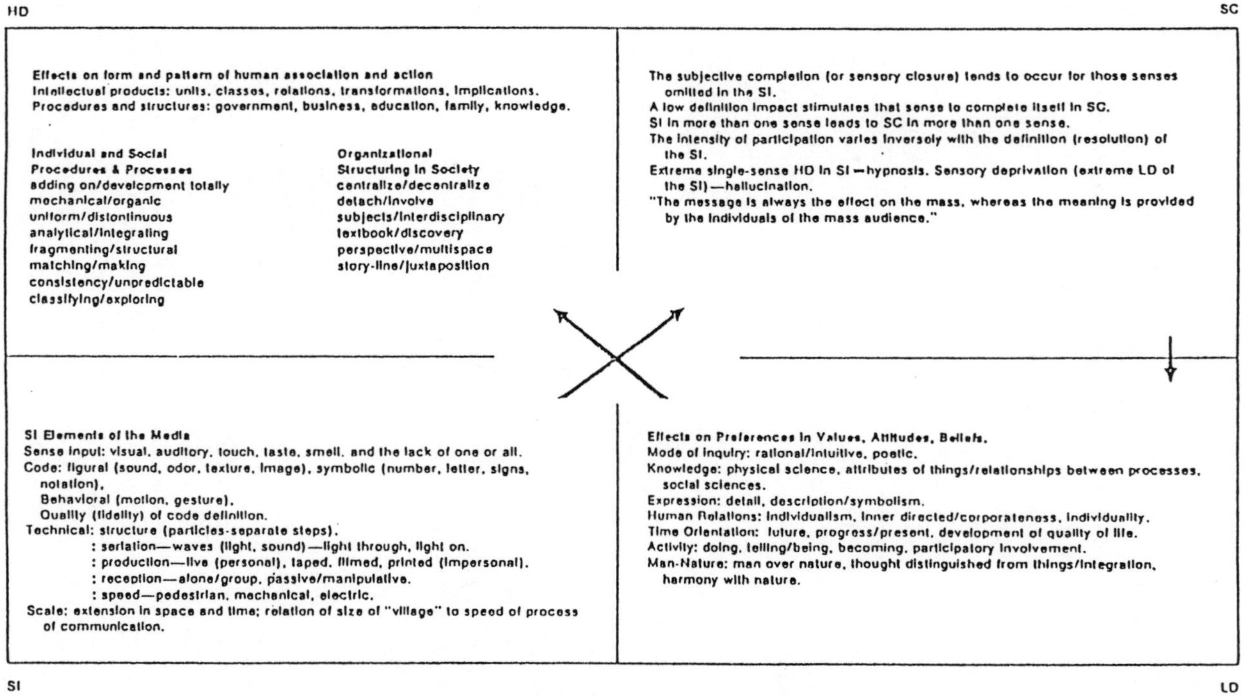

HD

Effects on form and pattern of human association and action
Intellectual products: units, classes, relations, transformations, implications.
Procedures and structures: government, business, education, family, knowledge.

Individual and Social
Procedures & Processes
adding on/development totally
mechanical/organic
uniform/distontinuous
analytical/integrating
fragmenting/structural
matching/making
consistency/unpredictable
classifying/exploring

Organizational
Structuring in Society
centralize/decentralize
detach/involve
subjects/interdisciplinary
textbook/discovery
perspective/multispace
story-line/juxtaposition

SC

The subjective completion (or sensory closure) tends to occur for those senses omitted in the SI.
A low definition impact stimulates that sense to complete itself in SC.
SI in more than one sense leads to SC in more than one sense.
The intensity of participation varies inversely with the definition (resolution) of the SI.
Extreme single-sense HD in SI — hypnosis. Sensory deprivation (extreme LD of the SI) — hallucination.
"The message is always the effect on the mass, whereas the meaning is provided by the individuals of the mass audience."

Effects on Preferences in Values, Attitudes, Beliefs.
Mode of Inquiry: rational/intuitive, poetic.
Knowledge: physical science, attributes of things/relationships between processes, social sciences.
Expression: detail, description/symbolism.
Human Relations: individualism, inner directed/corporateness, individuality.
Time Orientation: future, progress/present, development of quality of life.
Activity: doing, telling/being, becoming, participatory involvement.
Man-Nature: man over nature, thought distinguished from things/integration, harmony with nature.

SI Elements of the Media
Sense Input: visual, auditory, touch, taste, smell, and the lack of one or all.
Code: figural (sound, odor, texture, image), symbolic (number, letter, signs, notation).
Behavioral (motion, gesture).
Quality (fidelity) of code definition.
Technical: structure (particles-separate steps).
: seriation — waves (light, sound) — light through, light on.
: production — live (personal), taped, filmed, printed (impersonal).
: reception — alone/group, passive/manipulative.
: speed — pedestrian, mechanical, electric.
Scale: extension in space and time; relation of size of "village" to speed of process of communication.

SI

LD

Note: Characteristics of visual space are on the left of the slash / and those of acoustic space on the right, in the HD and LD sectors.

Source: Constructed by the author.

arrows to allow preferences and patterns to influence interpretation (SC). This changes the directional process and is no longer exactly as McLuhan initially saw it. However, if I am right in assuming that McLuhan's perception of what happens in 'subjective completion' or 'sensory closure' has itself become different, and that this area or activity is the "user's" interpretation of the message as well as the effect of the form of the message, then McLuhan can be seen to be taking into account the content and the medium both. This seems to be clearly stated in the letter to the *Globe and Mail*: "The message is always the effect on the mass, whereas the meaning is provided by the individuals of the mass audience" (McLuhan, 1972a). If the user is "interpreting" the message of media's forms as well as the meaning of the content, then he or she is in the position of the 'interpreter' in David K. Berlo's model of the process of communication (Ball and Byrnes, 1960). The SC is then more than sense reaction to achieve some balance; it is also interpretation of the meaning of the content of the message, and assimilation of the perception of the structure of the medium *as* a structure. This 'perception of structure' is conceptualized in the LD section of my chart (see Figure A.3) as cultural preferences, and these preferences are manifested as societal procedures and organizational patterns such as those listed in the HD section of the chart.

In fact, this version of the McLuhan charts is incomplete in its present format. There is a gap between the impact of the form of the medium and the resultant effects in SC and thence to LD and HD. These gaps are seen when the chart model is related to a slightly modified representation of Berlo's model (see Figure A.4). I have not shown interaction between the segments of this model, but the arrows in the central zone indicate one direction in which the process moves, that is, from stimulus to consequence to feedback. There is probably a flow back and forth between the parts of each segment, since a process involves all its elements, not isolating one from the others. It is possible to see how the receiver of a mediated message will be able to make meaning out of the "program" content because he or she understands and can decode the "language" in which the content message is couched. He might not realize he is also being affected by the form of the medium because he does not know the "grammars" of the media. It is also possible that the 'figure/ground' relationship, so prominent in McLuhan and Nevitt's *Take Today* (1972), is paralleled in the relationship between the inner and outer zones of each segment—the inner generally being the 'figure' (individual interpretation), and the outer being the 'ground' (effects on the cultural mass). Some might find a relationship here to general systems theory.

Having thus analyzed McLuhan's media charts and expanded them by relating them to the process of communication, there seems to be

Figure A.4
McLuhan's Chart Elements Extended by the Application of Berlo's Interpreter Model of the Process of Communication

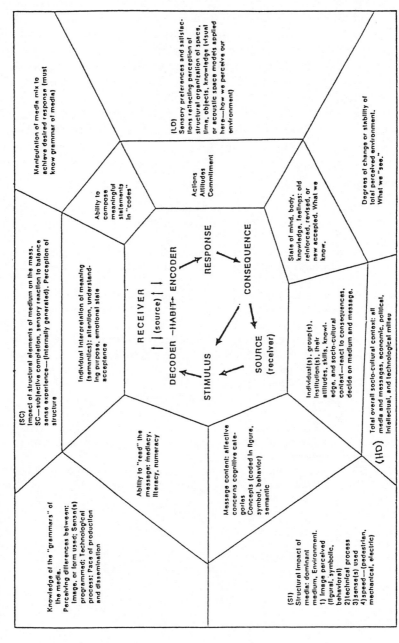

Source: Constructed by the author.

little in hand except questions. Do the various sectors of his model really match each other? Is the cultural perception of space, visual or acoustic, as dominantly important as it seems to be? What is visual space? Acoustic space? How much impact, and what kind of impact, do the technical factors really have? Are there alternative routes to McLuhan's conclusions? Such questions must be approached slowly; many people have answers that are useful, but these all have to be seen from within the confines of a model the construction of which may be nothing more than a funeral service for a powerful perception. On the other hand, as a potentially valid analogue of the communication process, it may have within it a certain power of its own. That remains to be seen.

NOTES

1. McLuhan's project was funded by Title VII of the U.S. National Defense Education Act and administered through the National Association of Educational Broadcasters.

2. "Image" is the word McLuhan uses. It denotes a visual perception. In this passage it includes perceptions of sound, touch, taste, and smell. This usage is a small example of a visually biased language.

3. From here on, citations solely by page number refer to McLuhan, 1960a.

4. It is interesting to note that the sentence quoted is omitted from the revised version of this article published in McLuhan's *DEW-LINE* newsletter (Nevitt, 1969). The charts remain the same. This may provide the answer to the question, in which case Nevitt has not followed the principle that an HD impact brings an SC of the omitted senses.

5. Paraphrased from McLuhan (1972b).

6. The peculiarities of McLuhan's style are illustrated in this quotation by his switch from "somewhat different" to "totally different." His method seemed to be to establish a reasonable position and then exaggerate it as a shock tactic to make it visible. This was fairly successful, but was perhaps no longer necessary once his aphorisms were familiar.

7. I have also depended to some extent on Kluckholn and Strodtbeck (1961) and on J. P. Guilford's structure of intellect model in *The Nature of Human Intelligence* (1967).

References

Alsberg, John. 1983. *Modern Art and Its Enigmas*. London: Weidenfeld and Nicolson.

Antoninus, Marcus Aurelius. 1906. *The Thoughts of Antoninus Marcus Aurelius*. Trans. by John Jackson. London: Oxford University Press.

Ausubel, D. P. 1964. "Some psychological aspects of the structure of knowledge," in S. Elam, ed., *Education and the Structure of Knowledge*. Chicago: Rand McNally, pp. 221–43.

Baldwin, Casey. 1977. "Interview with Professor Marshall McLuhan." *MacLean's*, 90:5, March 7, pp. 4–9.

Ball, J., and F. C. Byrnes, eds. 1960. *Research, Principles, and Practices in Visual Communication*. Washington, D.C.: National Education Association, Department of Audio Visual Instruction (now Association for Educational Communications and Technology), pp. 33–37.

Beaton, Alan. 1985. *Left Side, Right Side: A Review of Laterality Research*. London: Batsford Academic and Educational.

Beebe, Maurice. 1964. *Ivory Towers and Sacred Founts: The Artist as Hero in Fiction from Goethe to Joyce*. New York: New York University Press.

Bell, Ian F. A. 1981. *Critic as Scientist: The Modernist Poetics of Ezra Pound*. London: Methuen.

Benedict, Ruth. 1946. *The Chrysanthemum and the Sword: Patterns of Japanese Culture*. Boston: Houghton Mifflin.

Bergin, Thomas G., ed. 1966. *The Sonnets of Petrarch*. New York: Heritage Press.

Bergsten, Staffan. 1960. *Time and Eternity: A Study in the Structure and Symbolism of T. S. Eliot's "Four Quartets."* Bonniers, Stockholm: Svenska Bokförlaget.

Bevan, Edwyn R. 1936. "Rhetoric in the ancient world," in *Essays in Honour of Gilbert Murray*. London: George Allen and Unwin, pp. 189–213.

Bloom, Alfred H. 1981. *The Linguistic Shaping of Thought: A Study in the Impact of Language on Thinking in China and the West.* Hillsdale, N.J.: Laurence Erlbaum Associates.

Bogen, Joseph E. 1977. "Some educational implications of hemispheric specialization," in M. C. Wittrock, ed., *The Human Brain.* Englewood Cliffs, N.J.: Prentice-Hall, pp. 133–152.

Bogen, J. E., R. DeZure, W. D. Tenhouten, and J. F. Marsh. 1972. "The other side of the Brain, IV: The A/P ratio," *Bulletin of the Los Angeles Neurological Societies*, 37:2, April, pp. 49–61.

Bourdin, Alain. 1970. *McLuhan: Communication, Technologie, et Société.* Paris: Éditions Universitaires.

Bradshaw, John L., and Norman C. Nettleton. 1983. *Human Cerebral Asymmetry.* Englewood Cliffs, N.J.: Prentice-Hall (Century Psychology Series).

Cahill, James. 1982. *The Compelling Image: Nature and Style in Seventeenth-century Chinese Painting.* Cambridge, Mass.: Harvard University Press.

Capra, Fritjof. 1975. *The Tao of Physics: An Exploration of the Parallels between Modern Physics and Eastern Mysticism.* London: Wildwood House.

Carey, James W. 1981. "McLuhan and Mumford: the roots of modern media analysis." *Journal of Communication*, 31:3, Summer, pp. 162–78.

Castile, Rand. 1971. *The Way of Tea.* New York: Weatherhill.

Chaytor, H. J. 1945. *From Script to Print: An Introduction to Medieval Vernacular Literature.* Cambridge, England: W. Heffer and Sons.

Christy, Arthur. 1963 (1932). *The Orient in American Transcendentalism.* New York: Octagon Books.

Chu-Ming, Wong. 1963. "Commentary," in A. C. Crombie, ed., *Scientific Change: Historical Studies in the Intellectual, Social, and Technical Conditions for Scientific Discovery and Technical Invention, from Antiquity to the Present.* New York: Basic Books, pp. 166–67.

Code, Chris. 1987. *Language, Aphasia, and the Right Hemisphere.* Chichester, England: John Wiley & Sons.

Coleridge, Samuel Taylor. 1836 (1797). *The Poetical Works of S. T. Coleridge.* 3 Vols. London: William Pickering, vol. 1.

Collier, Peter. 1988. "The poetry of protest: Auden, Aragon, and Eluard," in Edward Timms and Peter Collier, eds., *Visions and Blueprints: Avant-garde Culture and Radical Politics in Early Twentieth Century Europe.* Manchester, England: Manchester University Press, pp. 137–58.

Corballis, Michael C. 1983. *Human Laterality.* New York: Academic Press.

Corn, Wanda M. 1973. *The Art of Andrew Wyeth.* Boston: New York Graphic Society.

Cort, David. 1966. "Any number can play." *New York Times Book Review*, May 1, pp. 6, 26.

Cowley, Abraham. 1707. "Davideis, a sacred poem of the troubles of David, Book I," in *The Works of Abraham of Cowley . . . ,* 10th ed. 2 Vols. London: printed for Jacob Tonson within Grays-Inn Gate next Grays-Inn Lane, vol. 1, pp. 287–320.

Crosby, Harry H., and George R. Bond. 1968. *The McLuhan Explosion: A Casebook on Marshall McLuhan and Understanding Media.* New York: American Book.

Culkin, John. 1989. "Marshall's New York adventure: reflections on McLuhan's year at Fordham University." in George Sanderson and Frank Macdonald, eds., *Marshall McLuhan: The Man and His Message*. Golden, Colo.: Fulcrum, pp. 99–110.

Curtis, James W. 1978. *Culture as Polyphony: An Essay on the Nature of Paradigms*. Columbia: University of Missouri Press.

Danto, Arthur. 1986. *The Philosophical Disenfranchisement of Art*. New York: Columbia University Press.

de Kerckhove, Derrick, and Charles J. Lumsden. 1988. "General conclusion," in Derrick de Kerckhove and Charles J. Lumsden, eds., *The Alphabet and the Brain: The Lateralization of Writing*. Berlin: Springer-Verlag, pp. 442–43.

DeFleur, Melvin L., and Sandra J. Ball-Rokeach. 1989. *Theories of Mass Communication*, 4 ed. New York: Longman.

Dervin, Brenda. 1981. "Mass communicating: changing conceptions of the audience," in Ronald E. Rice and William J. Paisely, eds., *Public Communication Campaigns*. Beverly Hills, Calif.: Sage Publications, pp. 71–87.

———. 1993. "An Overview of Sense-making Research: Concepts, Methods, and Results to Date." Presented at the International Communications Association Annual Meeting, Dallas, May.

Dervin, Brenda, and Michael Nilan. 1986. "Information needs and uses." *Annual Review of Information Science and Technology*, 21, pp. 3–33.

Drucker, Peter F. 1989. *The New Realities*. New York: Harper and Row.

Duffy, Dennis. 1969. *Marshall McLuhan*. Toronto: McLelland and Stewart.

Dumbrower, Julie, Jane Favero, William B. Michael, and Terri L. Cooper. 1981. "An attempt to determine the construct validity of measures hypothesized to represent an orientation to right, left, or integrated hemispheric brain function for a sample of primary school children." *Educational and Psychological Measurement*, 41:4, Winter, pp. 1175–94.

Dunaif-Hattis, Janet. 1984. *Doubling the Brain. On the Evolution of Brain Lateralization and Its Implications for Language*. New York: Peter Lang.

Eaman, Ross A. 1987. *The Media Society: Basic Issues and Controversies*. Toronto: Butterworths.

Edwards, Betty. 1979. *Drawing on the Right Side of the Brain*. Los Angeles: Tarcher.

Eisenstein, Elizabeth. 1979. *The Printing Press as an Agent of Change: Communications and Cultural Transformations in Early-modern Europe*. 2 Vols. Cambridge, England: Cambridge University Press.

Eliot, T. S. 1933. *The Use of Poetry and the Use of Criticism*. London: Faber and Faber.

———. 1941. *Points of View*. London: Faber and Faber.

———. 1948. *Notes towards the Definition of Culture*. London: Faber and Faber.

———. 1952. *The Complete Poems and Plays*. New York: Harcourt Brace, p. 117.

———. 1965. "What Dante means to me," in *To Criticize the Critic*. New York: Farrar Strauss and Giroux, pp. 125–35.

Emerson, R. W. N.d. "Nature," in *The Conduct of Life and Other Essays*. London: J. M. Dent (Everyman's Library), pp. 1–38.

Erasmus, D. 1961 (1511). "De ratione studii," in W. H. Woodward, ed., *Desiderius Erasmus concerning the Aim and Method of Education*. New York: Columbia University, Teachers College, Bureau of Publications.

Finkelstein, Sidney. 1968. *Sense and Nonsense of McLuhan*. New York: International Publishers.

Galland, Joseph S., and Roger Cros. 1931. *Nineteenth Century French Verse*. New York: Appleton-Century.

Gardner, Helen. 1978. *The Composition of "Four Quartets."* London: Faber and Faber.

Gazzaniga, Michael S. 1977. "Review of the split brain," in M. C. Wittrock, ed., *The Human Brain*. Englewood Cliffs, N.J.: Prentice-Hall, pp. 89–96.

Geschwind, Norman. 1972. "Language and the brain." *Scientific American*, 226:4, April, pp. 76–83.

Geschwind, Norman, and Walter Levitsky. 1968. "Human brain: left–right asymmetries in temporal speech regions." *Science*, 161:3837, July 12, pp. 186–87.

Giedion, Siegfried. 1948. *Mechanization Takes Command: A Contribution to Anonymous History*. New York: Oxford University Press.

Giles, Herbert A. 1915. *Confucianism and Its Rivals*. London: Williams and Norgate.

Glenn, Edmund S., and Christine G. Glenn. 1981. *Man and Mankind: Conflict and Communication between Cultures*. Norwood, N.J.: Ablex Publishing.

Goldberg, Toby. 1971. "An examination, critique, and evaluation of the mass communications theories of Marshall McLuhan." Ann Arbor, Mich.: UMI Research Press, pp. 71–20, 664 (Ph.D. dissertation, University of Wisconsin, 1971).

Goldwater, Robert, and Marco Treves. 1947. *Artists on Art*, 2nd rev. ed. New York: Pantheon Books.

Graham, A. C. 1989. *Disputers of the Tao: Philosophical Argument in Ancient China*. LaSalle, Ill.: Open Court.

Grassi, Ernesto. 1983. *Heidegger and the Question of Renaissance Humanism*. Binghamton: Center for Medieval and Early Renaissance Studies, State University of New York at Binghamton.

Gray, William S., and Ruth Munroe. 1929. *The Reading Interests and Habits of Adults*. New York: Macmillan.

Guilford, J. P. 1967. *The Nature of Human Intelligence*. New York: McGraw-Hill.

Hall, David L., and Roger T. Ames. 1987. *Thinking Through Confucius*. Albany, N.Y.: State University of New York Press.

Hay, John. 1974. *Masterpieces of Chinese Art*. London: Phaidon.

Henry, Nelson B., ed. 1956. *Adult Reading. The Fifty-fifth Yearbook of the National Society for the Study of Education. Part II*. Chicago: National Society for the Study of Education.

Hiscock, Merrill, and Marcel Kinsbourne. 1987. "Specialization of the cerebral hemispheres: implications for learning." *Journal of Learning Disabilities*, 20:3, March, pp. 130–43.

Holorenshaw, Henry. 1973. "The making of an honorary Taoist," in Mikulás Teich and Robert Young, eds., *Changing Perspectives in the History of Science: Essays in Honour of Joseph Needham*. London: Heinemann Educational, pp. 1–20.

Howard, Jane. 1966. "Oracle of the electric age." *Life*, February 28, pp. 91–99.

Hu Shih. 1963 (1922). *The Development of the Logical Method in Ancient China*. New York: Paragon Book Reprint (first edition, Shanghai, 1922).

Hughes, Robert. 1980. *The Shock of the New: Art and the Century of Change*. London: British Broadcasting.

Hurst, W. A. 1981. "Vision, brain hemispheres, learning disabilities," *Contacto* (United States), 25:1, January, pp. 30–40.

Innis, H. A. 1951. *The Bias of Communication*. Toronto: University of Toronto Press.

Ito, Youichi. 1989. "A non-Western view of the paradigm dialogues," in Brenda Dervin et al., eds., *Rethinking Communication*, Vol. 1: *Paradigm Issues*. Newbury Park, Calif.: Sage Publications, pp. 173–77.

James, William. 1890. *The Principles of Psychology*. 2 Vols. New York: Holt, vol. 2.

Jaynes, Julian. 1977. *The Origin of Consciousness in the Breakdown of the Bicameral Mind*. Boston: Houghton Mifflin.

Johnson, Paul. 1991. *The Birth of the Modern: World Society 1815–1830*. New York: HarperCollins.

Johnson-Laird, P. N., and P. C. Wason, eds. 1977. *Thinking: Readings in Cognitive Science*. Cambridge, England: Cambridge University Press.

Jonson, Ben. 1946. "Timber: or discoveries made upon men and matter," in Robert P. Tristram Coffin and Alexander W. Witherspoon, eds., *Seventeenth Century Prose and Poetry*. New York: Harcourt Brace, pp. 125–42 (a selection).

Joyce, James. 1968. *A Portrait of the Artist as a Young Man*. New York: Penguin Books (first published serially in 1915; first published in the United States in 1916).

Judson, Horace Freeland. 1980. *The Search for Solutions*. New York: Holt, Rinehart, and Winston.

Katz, Solomon H. 1975. "Toward a new science of humanity." *Zygon*, 10:1, March, pp. 12–31.

Kennedy, John M. 1973. *A Psychology of Picture Perception*. San Francisco: Jossey-Bass.

Kierkegaard, Soren. 1944 (1844). *Concept of Dread*. Trans. by Walter Lowrie. Princeton, N.J.: Princeton University Press.

Kiminye, Barbara. 1966. *Kalasanda Revisited*. London: Oxford.

Kluckholn, R. R., and F. L. Strodtbeck, 1961. *Variations in Value Orientations*. Evanston, Ill.: Row, Peterson.

Kostelanetz, Richard. 1968. "A Hot apostle in a cool culture," in Robert Rosenthal, ed., *McLuhan: Pro and Con*. New York: Funk and Wagnalls, pp. 207–28.

Krugman, Herbert E. 1970. "Electro-encephalographic aspects of low involvement: implications for the McLuhan hypothesis," paper delivered to the American Association for Public Opinion Research, Hotel Sagamore, Lake George, N.Y., May 21–23.

———. 1971. "Brain wave measures of media involvement." *Journal of Advertising Research*, 11:1, February, pp. 3–9.

———. 1978. "The two brains: new evidence," paper delivered at the Advertising Research Foundation Annual Conference, October 16.

Kuhns, William. 1989. "A McLuhan symposium," in George Sanderson and Frank Macdonald, eds., *Marshall McLuhan: The Man and His Message*. Golden, Colo.: Fulcrum, pp. 111–20.

Kwok, Daniel W. Y. 1965. *Scientism in Chinese Thought, 1900–1950*. New Haven, Conn.: Yale University Press.

Leavis, F. R., ed. 1970 (1933). *Towards Standards of Criticism: Selections from* The Calendar of Modern Letters, 1925–1927. Folcroft, Pa.: Folcroft (first published by Wishart, 1933).

Leavis, Q. D. 1965 (c. 1932). *Fiction and the Reading Public*. New York: Russell and Russell.

Levy, Jerre. 1974. "Psychobiological implications of bilateral asymmetry," in J. G. Beaumont and S. J. Diamond, eds., *Hemisphere Function in the Human Brain*. London: Elek, pp. 121–83.

Lewis, C. Day. 1956. *Enjoying Poetry: A Reader's Guide*, 3rd ed. Cambridge, England: Cambridge University Press.

Lewis, C. S. 1961. *An Experiment in Criticism*. Cambridge, England: Cambridge University Press.

Lewis, Percy Wyndham. 1971. *Wyndham Lewis the Artist: From "Blast" to Burlington House*. New York: Haskell House Publications.

Lieberman, Ben. 1967. "Paradise regained or McLuhanacy," in Gerald Emanuel Stearn, ed., *McLuhan: Hot and Cool*. New York: New American Library, pp. 21–224.

Lievrouw, Leah A., and T. Andrew Finn. 1990. "Identifying the common dimensions of communication: the communication systems model," in Brent D. Ruben and Leah A. Lievrouw, eds., *Mediation, Information, and Communication: Information and Behavior*. New Brunswick, N.J.: Transaction Publishers, vol. 3, pp. 37–65.

Littlejohn, Stephen W. 1989. *Theories of Human Communication*, 3d ed. Belmont, Calif.: Wadsworth Publishing.

Louie, Kam. 1980. *Critiques of Confucius in Contemporary China*. New York: St. Martin's Press.

Luria, A. K. 1970. "The functional organization of the brain." *Scientific American*, 222:3, March, pp. 66–78.

McGann, Jerome J. 1988. "The Cantos of Ezra Pound, the truth in contradiction." *Critical Inquiry*, 15:1, Autumn, pp. 1–25.

MacLeish, Archibald. 1926. "Ars Poetica." *Poetry*, 28:3, June, pp. 126–27.

McLuhan, Marshall. 1950. "Pound's critical prose," in Peter Russell, ed., *An Examination of Ezra Pound*. Norfolk, Conn.: New Directions, pp. 165–71.

———. 1951. *The Mechanical Bride: Folklore of Industrial Man*. New York: Vanguard.

———. 1953. "Culture without literacy." *Explorations*, 1, December, pp. 117–27.

———. 1955. Article written for *Explorations*, 4, p. 56.

———. 1957. Personal correspondence, March 14.

———. 1960a. *Report on Project in Understanding New Media*. Report No. 7A–279, U.S. Office of Education. ERIC Doc. No. ED 017–166.

———. 1960b. "Electronics and the changing role of print." *AV Communication Review*, 8:5, Supplement 2, pp. 74–83.

———. 1962. *The Gutenberg Galaxy: The Making of Typographic Man*. Toronto: University of Toronto Press.

————. 1964a. "Introduction," in H. A. Innis, *The Bias of Communication*. Toronto: University of Toronto Press (1951; 1964 reprint).

————. 1964b. *Understanding Media: The Extensions of Man*. New York: McGraw-Hill.

————. 1968a. *Through the Vanishing Point: Space in Poetry and Painting*. New York: Harper.

————. 1968b. *War and Peace in the Global Village*. New York: Bantam.

————.1969. "The aesthetic moment in landscape poetry," in E. McNamara, ed., *The Interior Landscape: The Literary Criticism of Marshall McLuhan, 1943–1962*. New York: McGraw-Hill, pp. 157–67.

————. 1970a. *Culture Is Our Business*. New York: McGraw-Hill.

————. 1970b. "Libraries: past, present, future," speech delivered at the State University of New York at Geneseo, July.

————. 1972a. Letter. Toronto *Globe and Mail*, March 4, p. 7.

————. 1972b. Personal correspondence. March 10.

————. 1972c. Untitled handout. Toronto, Center for Culture and Technology, University of Toronto.

————. 1974. Personal correspondence, June 28.

————. 1975. "McLuhan's laws of the media." *Journal of Technology and Culture*, 16:1, January, pp. 74–78.

————. 1976. "Understanding the media's laws." *Technology and Culture*, 17:2, April, p. 263.

————. 1978. "The brain and the media: the 'Western Hemisphere.' " *Journal of Communication*, 28:4, Autumn, pp. 54–60.

McLuhan, Marshall, and Eric McLuhan. 1974. "Gesetze der Medien Strukturelle Annäherung," in *Unitericht-swisserschaft*. Berlin: Beltz Berlag Sonderdruck, pp. 79–84.

————. 1988. *Laws of Media: The New Science*. Toronto: University of Toronto Press.

McLuhan, Marshall, and Barrington Nevitt. 1972. *Take Today: The Executive as Dropout*. Don Mills, Ontario: Longman Canada.

McLuhan, Marshall, and Bruce R. Powers. 1989. *The Global Village: Transformations in World Life and Media in the 21st Century*. New York: Oxford University Press.

McLuhan, Marshall, and Wilfred Watson. 1970. *From Cliché to Archetype*. New York: Viking.

McNamara, Eugene, ed. 1969. *The Interior Landscape: The Literary Criticism of Marshall McLuhan, 1943–1962*. New York: McGraw-Hill.

Madsen, Richard. 1984. *Morality and Power in a Chinese Village*. Berkeley: University of California Press.

Mallarmé, Stéphane. 1920. *Vers et Prose*. Paris: Perrin et Cie.

Manchester, William. 1988. *The Last Lion: Winston Spencer Churchill: Alone, 1932–1940*. Boston: Little, Brown.

Marchand, Philip. 1989. *Marshall McLuhan: The Medium and the Messenger*. Toronto: Random House.

Millar, Janice M., and Harry A. Whitaker. 1983. "The right hemisphere's contribution to language: a review of the evidence from brain-damaged subjects," in S. J. Segalowitz, ed., *Language Functions and Brain Organization*. London: Academic Press, pp. 87–113.

Miller, George A., and David McNeil. 1969. "Psycholinguistics," in Gardner Lindzey and Elliot Aronson, eds., *The Handbook of Social Biology*, 2nd ed. Reading, Mass.: Addison-Wesley, vol. 3, pp. 666–794.

Miller, Jonathan. 1971. *Marshall McLuhan*. New York: Viking Press (Modern Masters Series).

Mokyr, Joel. 1990. *The Lever of Riches: Technological Creativity and Economic Progress*. New York: Oxford University Press.

Molinaro, Matie, Corinne McLuhan, and William Toye, eds. 1987. *Letters of Marshall McLuhan*. Toronto: Oxford University Press.

Morton, W. Scott. 1980. *China: Its History and Culture*. New York: Lippincott and Crowell.

Mukerji, Chandra. 1983. *From Graven Images: Patterns of Modern Materialism*. New York: Columbia University Press.

Murdoch, Dugald. 1987. *Niels Bohr's Philosophy of Physics*. Cambridge, England: Cambridge University Press.

Needham, Joseph. 1963. "Poverties and triumphs of the Chinese scientific tradition," in A. C. Crombie, ed., *Scientific Change: Historical Studies in the Intellectual, Social, and Technical Invention, from Antiquity to the Present*. New York: Basic Books, pp. 117–53.

————. 1965. *Time and Eastern Man*. Glasgow, Scotland: Royal Anthropological Institute of Great Britain and Ireland.

Needham, Joseph, assisted by Wang Ling, Kenneth Robinson, Ho Ping-Yii, and Lu Gwei-Djin. 1954–86. *Science and Civilization in China*. Cambridge, England: Cambridge University Press.

Needham, Joseph, Wang Ling, and Derek de Solla Price. 1960. *Heavenly Clockwork: The Great Astronomical Clocks of Medieval China*. Cambridge, England: Cambridge University Press (2 ed. 1986).

Neill, S. D. 1964. "Understanding media." Letter on *Understanding Media* (by Marshall McLuhan, New York: McGraw-Hill, 1964). Toronto *Globe and Mail*, August 7, p. 6.

————. 1971. "Books and Marshall McLuhan." *Library Quarterly*, 41:4, pp. 311–19.

————. 1973a. "McLuhan's media charts related to the process of communication." *AV Communication Review*, 21:3, Fall, pp. 277–97.

————. 1973b. Review of *Take Today: The Executive as Dropout* (by Marshall McLuhan and Barrington Nevitt, New York: Harcourt Brace Jovanovich, 1972). *Library Quarterly*, 43:2, April, pp. 170–72.

Nevitt, Barrington. 1967. "Problems of communicating with people through media." *The* (Ottawa, Canada, Northern Electric Research and Development Laboratories), no. 1.

————. 1969. Revised version of "Problems of communicating with people through media." *DEW-LINE*, March, sec. 1 (unpaged).

————. 1973. Personal correspondence, January.

————. 1981. "Archivist and comprehensivist." *Argus*, 10:3–4, August, pp. 65–70.

————. 1982. *The Communication Ecology*. Toronto: Butterworths.

Okakura-Kakuzo. 1912. *The Book of Tea*. New York: Duffield.

Ong, Walter J. 1982. *Orality and Literacy: The Technologizing of the Word*. London: Methuen.

Palgrave, Francis Turner. 1964. *The Golden Treasury*, 5th ed. London: Oxford University Press.

Pearce, W. Barnett, and Vernon E. Cronen. 1980. *Communication, Action, and Meaning: The Creation of Social Realities*. New York: Praeger.

Peel, Robert. 1946. Review of *The Chrysanthemum and the Sword* (by Ruth Benedict, Boston: Houghton Mifflin, 1946). *Christian Science Monitor*, December 16, p. 16.

Petrarca, Francesco. 1879 (14th century). *The Sonnets, Triumphs, and Other Poems of Petrarch. Now first completely translated into English verse by various hands. With a life of the poet by Thomas Campbell*. London: George Bell and Sons.

Pollak, Richard. 1966. "Understanding McLuhan." *Newsweek*, February 28, pp. 56–57.

Popper, Karl R. 1972. *Objective Knowledge: An Evolutionary Approach*. Oxford, England: Oxford University Press.

Pound, Ezra. N.d. (1934). *ABC of Reading*. Norfolk, Conn.: New Directions.

———. 1954a. "The serious artist," in T. S. Eliot, ed., *Literary Essays of Ezra Pound*. London: Faber and Faber, pp. 41–57.

———. 1954b. "T. S. Eliot," in T. S. Eliot, ed., *Literary Essays of Ezra Pound*. London: Faber and Faber, pp. 418–22.

———. 1954c. "The teacher's mission," in T. S. Eliot, ed., *Literary Essays of Ezra Pound*. London: Faber and Faber, pp. 58–63 (first published in the *English Journal*, 1934).

———. 1954d. Essay on Henry James, in T. S. Eliot, ed., *Literary Essays of Ezra Pound*. London: Faber and Faber, p. 297 (first published in the *Little Review*, 4, August 1918, pp. 5–9).

Powe, B. W. 1984. *A Climate Charged*. Oakville, Canada: Mosaic Press.

Powers, Bruce. 1981. "Final thoughts: a collaborator on Marshall's methods and meanings." *Journal of Communication*, 31:3, Summer, pp. 189–90.

Read, Herbert. 1948. *Form in Modern Poetry*. London: Vision Press.

Reibetanz, Julia Maniates. 1983. *A Reading of Eliot's "Four Quartets."* Ann Arbor, Mich.: UMI Research Press.

Richards, I. A. 1929. *Practical Criticism: A Study of Literary Judgment*. London: K. Paul, Trench, Trubner.

Richards, I. A., and C. K. Ogden. 1923. *The Meaning of Meaning*. London: K. Paul, Trench, Trubner.

Rubin, Edgar. 1958. "Figure and ground," in David C. Beardslee and Michael Wertheimer, eds., *Readings in Perception*. Princeton, N.J.: D. Van Nostrand, pp. 194–203 (Rubin's piece c. 1915).

Sanderson, George, and Frank Macdonald, eds. 1989. *Marshall McLuhan: The Man and His Message*. Golden, Colo.: Fulcrum.

Scholes, Robert. 1989. *Protocols of Reading*. New Haven, Conn.: Yale University Press.

Schramm, Wilbur. 1954. *The Process and Effects of Mass Communication*. Urbana: University of Illinois Press.

Schwartz, Tony. 1973. *The Responsive Chord*. Garden City, N.Y.: Anchor Press.

Severin, Werner J., and James W. Tankard, Jr. 1988. *Communication Theories: Origins, Methods, Uses*, 2 ed. New York: Longman.

Shakespeare, William. *Coriolanus*. N.d. London and Glasgow: William Collins.

————. 1904 (1606). *Macbeth*. Ed. by Thomas Marc Parrott. New York: American Book.

————. 1969 (17th century). *Troilus and Cressida*. Ed. by Arthur Quiller-Couch. Cambridge, England: Cambridge University Press.

Shannon, Claude E., and Warren Weaver. 1949. *The Mathematical Theory of Communication*. Urbana: University of Illinois Press.

Shapiro, Karl. *A Primer for Poets*. 1953. Lincoln: University of Nebraska Press.

Shelley, Percy Bysshe. 1976 (1821). *Shelley's "Defence of Poetry" and Blunden's Lectures on "Defence."* Norwood, Pa.: Norwood Editions, pp. 17–71 (written in 1821; published first in 1840).

Smith, Edward L. *The Body in Psychotherapy*. 1985. Jefferson, N.C.: McFarland.

Smith, John. 1978. *The Arts Betrayed*. London: Herbert Press.

Stanovich, Keith E. 1988. "Explaining the differences between the dyslexic and the garden-variety poor reader: the phonological—core variable—difference model." *Journal of Learning Disabilities*, 21:10, December, pp. 590–604.

Stearn, Gerald E. 1967. "A dialogue: Q & A," in Gerald Emanuel Stearn, ed., *McLuhan: Hot and Cool*. New York: New American Library, pp. 259–92.

Steiner, George. 1975. *After Babel: Aspects of Language and Translation*. New York: Oxford University Press.

Steinfatt, Thomas M. 1989. "Linguistic relativity: toward a broader view," in Stella Ting-Toomey and Felipe Korzenny, eds., *Language, Communication, and Culture: Current Directions*. Newbury Park, Calif.: Sage Publications, pp. 35–75.

Strauss, Harold. 1946. Review of *The Chrysanthemum and the Sword* (by Ruth Benedict, Boston: Houghton Mifflin, 1946). *New York Times Book Review*, November 24, p. 4.

Sturrock, John. 1989. "Wild man of the global village." Review of *Laws of Media: The New Science* (by Marshall McLuhan and Eric McLuhan, Toronto: University of Toronto Press, 1988). *New York Times Book Review*, February 26, p. 39.

Taylor, Insup. 1988. "Psychology of literacy: East and West," in Derrick de Kerckhove and Charles J. Lumsden, eds., *The Alphabet and the Brain: The Lateralization of Writing*. Berlin: Springer-Verlag, pp. 202–33.

Teich, Mikulás, and Robert Young. 1973. "Introduction," in Mikulás Teich and Robert Young, eds., *Changing Perspectives in the History of Science: Essays in Honour of Joseph Needham*. London: Heinemann Educational, pp. ix–xxi.

Tejera, Victorino. 1965. *Art and Human Intelligence*. New York: Appleton-Century-Crofts.

Theall, Donald F. 1971. *The Medium Is the Rear-view Mirror: Understanding McLuhan*. Montreal: McGill–Queen's University Press.

Trevarthen, Colwyn. 1983. "Development of the cerebral mechanism for language," in Ursula Kirk, ed., *Neuropsychology of Language, Reading and Spelling*. New York: Academic Press, pp. 45–80.

Trotsky, Leon. 1960 (1924). *Literature and Revolution*. Ann Arbor: University of Michigan Press.

Trotter, R. J. 1976. "The other hemisphere." *Science News*, 109:14, April 3, pp. 218–20, 223.

Tzeng, Ovid J. L., and Daisy L. Hung. 1988. "Orthography, reading, and cerebral functions," in Derrick de Kerckhove and Charles J. Lumsden, eds., *The Alphabet and the Brain: The Lateralization of Writing.* Berlin: Springer-Verlag, pp. 273–90.

Venable, William Henry. 1976. pp. 256–62. "Flaws in McLuhan's laws." *Technology and Culture*, 17:2, April, pp. 256–62.

Wagner, Geoffrey. 1957. *Wyndham Lewis: A Portrait of the Artist as the Enemy.* New Haven, Conn.: Yale University Press.

Waples, Douglas, Bernard Berelson, and F. W. Bradshaw. 1940. *What Reading Does to People.* Chicago: University of Chicago Press.

Watzlawick, P., J. H. Beavin, and D. D. Jackson. 1967. *Pragmatics of Human Communication.* New York: W. W. Norton.

White, Lynn, Jr. 1962. *Medieval Technology and Social Change.* Oxford, England: Clarendon Press.

Whorf, Benjamin Lee. 1956. *Language, Thought, and Reality: Selected Writings.* Cambridge, Mass.: MIT Press.

Witkin, Herman A. 1978. *Cognitive Styles in Personal and Cultural Adaptation.* Worcester, Mass.: Clark University Press.

Wordsworth, William. 1891. "Lines composed a few miles above Tintern Abbey, on revisiting the banks of the Wye during a tour, July 13, 1798," in *Lyrical Ballads*, 2nd ed. Ed. by Edward Dowden. London, David Nutt.

Yee, Chiang. 1964. *The Chinese Eye: An Interpretation of Chinese Painting.* Bloomington: Indiana University Press.

Zukerman, Eugenia. 1989. "The cold hands of genius." Review of *Glenn Gould: A Life and Variations* (by Otto Friedrich, New York: Random House, 1989). *New York Times Book Review*, April 23, p. 22.

Name Index

Subject Index

About the Author

S. D. NEILL was Professor at the School of Library and Information Science, University of Western Ontario. Among his earlier publications is *Dilemmas in the Study of Information* (Greenwood Press, 1988).